THE IMPROV WORKSHOP HANDBOOK

*Creative Movement and Verbal Interaction
for Students K-8*

~The Object Is Teamwork~

by

Milton E. Polsky

and

Jack Gilead

Illustrations by

Richard Rockwell

PLAYERS PRESS, Inc.

P. O. Box 1132
Studio City, CA 91614-0132

THE IMPROV WORKSHOP HANDBOOK
Creative Movement and Verbal Interaction for Students K-8
~The Object Is Teamwork~
© Copyright, 2001, by Milton Polsky and Players Press, Inc.

Simultaneously Published in
U.S.A., U.K., Canada and Australia

Printed in the U.S.A.

Editor: Chris Cordero
Book Layout and Paste-Up: Chris Cordero
Typeset: Judith Horsley and Chris Cordero
Catalogue: Wendy Landes

From GREAT ACTION GAMES FOR CREATIVE MOVEMENT by Milton Polsky and Jack Gilead. © Copyright by The Instructor Publications, Inc. Reprinted by permission of Scholastic.

Library of Congress-Cataloging-in-Publication Data

Polsky, Milton E.
   The improv workshop handbook : creative movement and verbal interaction for students K-8 / by Milton E. Polsky and Jack Gilead ; illustrations by Richard Rockwell.
      p. cm.
   ISBN 0-88734-691-X
      1. Improvisation (Acting) 2. Movement education. 3. Interpersonal communication--Study and teaching (Elementary)--Activity programs. I. Gilead, Jack. II. Title.

PN2071.I5 P64 2002
792'.028--dc21

2002016940

CONTENTS

FOREWORD

The size of this text is very deceptive, for in its compactness it contains one of the most extensive array of ideas for improvisation I have ever seen. It is an extremely useful handbook that should help the teacher/director bring improvisation, theatre games, movement, and language arts together in a working harmony with the young player/student and the learning environment.

The theme of the book, "Teamwork", introduced in Part One is carried out in every chapter and activity. The theatre, after all, is an art form in which many work together, and the more cooperative they are, the better. The integration of creative movement and verbal literacy tightens the focus of the book so that it completes the process of improvisation. For Professor Polsky, an experienced teacher, is not simply providing readers with appealing leisure time activities but is giving them ways of including movement and the language arts through the medium of theatre techniques.

The second part of the book is divided into five sections, each with a focus on a particular aspect of a subject such as "Let's Move!", "Say It In Silence" and "Speak Up!" What I suspect will be the greatest value to teachers are ideas for follow-up. Dr. Polsky furthermore includes all of the arts in this part, suggesting the most appropriate to the subject matter and to the age of the students. Beyond the fun that the players will have with this handbook is its solid educational base. Inexperienced teachers will find additional help in the extensions that are included in every lesson. While directed to younger children, the book is appropriate for all ages. The pages are amply provided with illustrations that complement and enhance the text. There are several good books on creative drama on the market but this book is unique in its thrust and format.

Nellie McCaslin
Program in Educational Theatre
New York University

INTRODUCTION
Run Like A River

Creative movement, group pantomime, and verbal games are enjoyable forms of improvisational drama.

Through creative movement, individuals—alone or with others—apply a variety of vivid images to express themselves. As arms stretch out to become a river, the mind does a dance—what kind of river is this, how does it move? What does it look like? How does it sound?

As the river opens up and begins to flow, the movers "let themselves go" within a structured framework of self-control. They begin to open up, lose their inhibitions and free their powers of concentration. Imaginations now become more free to communicate diverse feelings and ideas.

Through group pantomime, individuals work together to create memorable images with their bodies. Who or what is in the river—a swimmer, fish or gigantic whale? Who is doing what—and why? Is the river clean or polluted, and how can this be shown silently?

A special form of group pantomime is the focus of Part One, "The Object Is Teamwork." Using cooperative learning skills, students are challenged to create with their bodies such familiar objects as clocks and musical instruments—and more fantastic ones such as "The Quintessence of Quiet."

Each session invites the reader to think about the problem involved in becoming the object; discovering how to solve the problem; and solving the problem. The session concludes with art and language arts follow-up activities.

Because the games in Part One always involve students working in groups, teamwork is especially important. In most cases, group members are happy to support each other to create something they can be proud of. The nice thing about teamwork is that there are always people on your side ready to help.

The follow-up activities in Part One help students to explore more curricular ways to enrich the drama activity—so that, like a river, the activity can run its full course.

The Second Part of this book, "Creating With More Movement and Verbal Games" helps students to explore—silently and with words—many familiar and fantastic worlds, from becoming "invisible" moving microbes to enacting a delicate Japanese tea ceremony. Each game has a clearly stated objective and a "Try This" extension activity.

Using movement, pantomime and speaking skills learned in Part Two will help students to expand their abilities to learn more about drama and life. They will enjoy enacting short plays and scenes such as everyday situations, historical highlights, and language concepts.

Along with movement and mime, verbal games promote all kinds of learning. Students learn to express their inner thoughts and to speak up in order to communicate their ideas. When young people link their ideas with each other, there is, like a river, a tremendous flow of positive energy, and creativity is discovered anew.

Have fun on your creative journeys!

Milton Polsky

Ten Tips for Working Together

Planning
1. Listen to each other's ideas.
2. Talk *one at a time*. You'll get more done.
3. Be respectful of each other's ideas and person.
4. Say "Here's another idea" instead of "My idea is better."
5. Tie ideas together when possible until you have one that works.
6. Be prepared to do some parts over if they're not clear.

Revising
7. Ask:
   - How did the team show imagination?
   - How did the team show teamwork?
   - Give examples of how the team communicated its efforts.
8. Expect the unexpected—if something works, use it. Revise for clarity and interest.
9. *Focus* on what you're trying to accomplish. Keep your plan or *framework* clear. Go with the *flow* of the team.
10. Remember: If you're not in it, you can't win it. When you work together, you win together!

Guiding Groups
Tips for the Teacher and Workshop Leader

Role of the Teacher/Leader
The role of any leader in creative team endeavors is to inspire, motivate, and guide participants so that they can best actualize their own creativity.

Guiding Development
One of the primary goals of good leadership is to provide questions with which the players can make discoveries on their own. For example, instead of saying, "I want you to be a wheel in a machine," it is better to ask the player, "What are you doing in the machine?" "What do you want as the wheel?" "How do you feel about it?" Help students find their own focus and framework of development.

Guiding for Refinement
A creative leader recognizes the importance of revision. He or she realizes that a balance often evolves between conscious deliberation about the problem and the spontaneous combustion of ideas that occur during planning, playing, and refining stages. Ask: How is what you're planning, presenting, and refining imaginative and clear?

As refining guideposts, encourage students to ask, for example, such questions as:
- How can we make this clearer?
- How can we work more effectively in our group?

Growing in Groups
Groups need encouragement and a sense of success—things that you, as a leader, can help generate by providing a warm, supportive environment with well-focused discipline.

What the players create will, in most cases, come from their collective and individual experience, so it can never be really "wrong." It may be merely something you did not have in mind. Therefore, it is important that you not impose your ideas on the work of the team or individual concerned. If this happens, the joy of the creative process is taken away, and players are cheated out of the meaningful learning experience of thinking through a problem and experimenting with a solution.

Good luck with your program and creative leadership! And remember: process can be your best product!

Part One
~The Object Is Teamwork~

Become An Airplane

Think About It

Look at the airplanes on the facing page. What things do they have in common? Discuss how it might feel if *you* were an airplane flying in the sky. What are some positive things that air flight accomplishes?

Let's Find Out

1. Get together in teams consisting of 6-8 players.
2. One or two of you become *wings*; some more, the *propeller* or *jets*; and one, the plane's *tail*. You'll also need some *passengers* and a *pilot*.
3. Make sure you connect all the parts in the right order.

Solve the Problem

How can you make your plane move? As the plane moves around the space, you and your friends can take turns saying how it feels to be flying so peacefully in the sky.

Follow-up Activities

• Become different kinds of planes.
• Land in a specific, happy place, become visitors and people who live there, and make up a little scene.

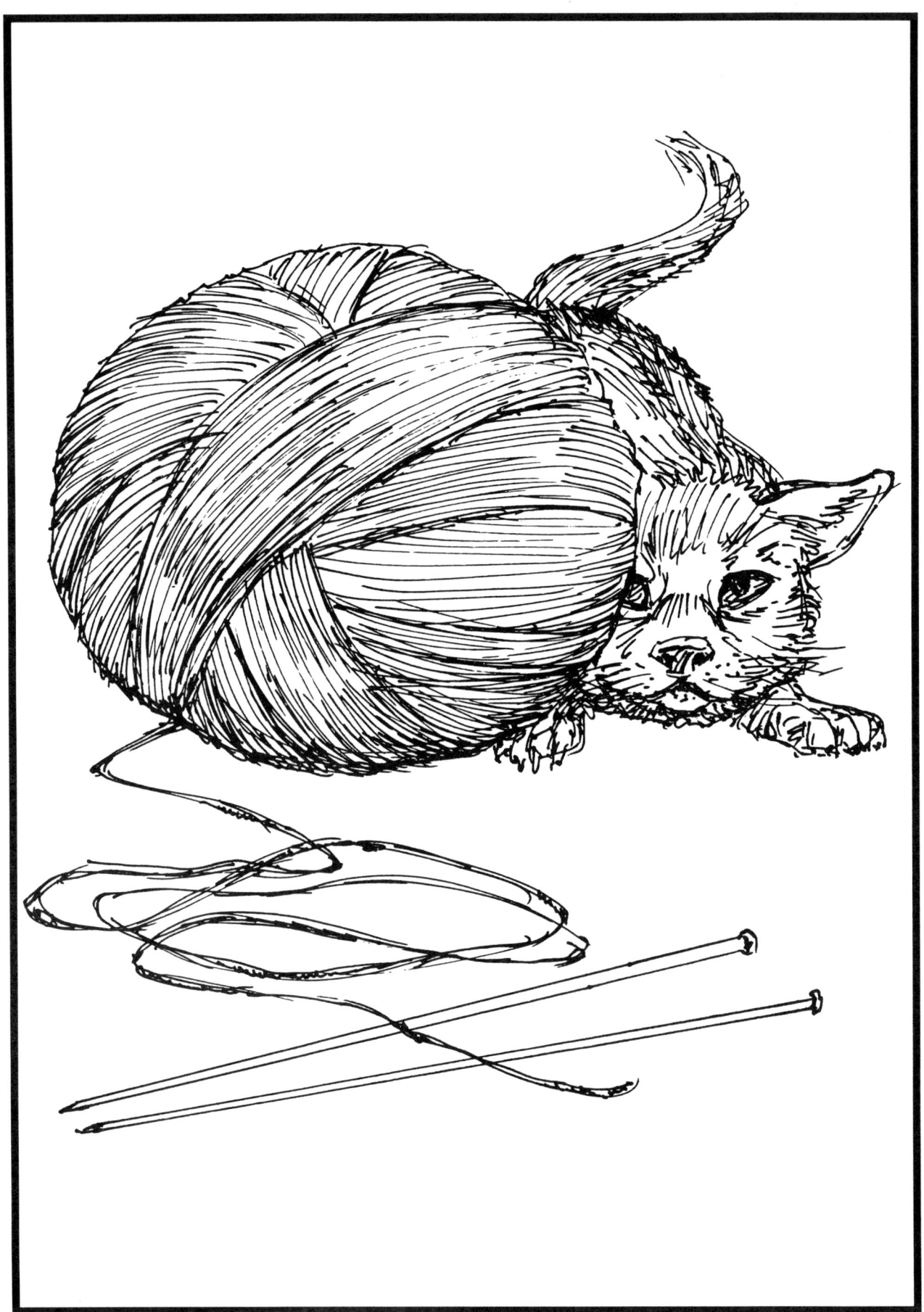

Become A Ball Of Yarn

Think About It

Look at the picture of a ball of yarn on the facing page. What kinds of things does it make you think of? Share your thoughts. How do you think it would feel if *you* became a ball of yarn?

Let's Find Out

1. Make a small circle consisting of five to seven players.
2. Every player should extend one arm forward and move s-l-o-w-l-y toward the center of the circle.
3. Each player *gently* grasps *one* free hand of another player, so that every hand is being held by only one other hand.
4. You have created a twisty ball of yarn!

Solve the Problem

See if you can unravel the ball without breaking the thread— the grasp of each other's hands. (It can be done!)

Follow-up Activities

• Try making balls of yarn with different combinations of people.
• With another team of players, create a GIANT scissors to "cut through" another team's ball of yarn.

Become A Clock

Think About It

Look at the different clocks on the facing page. What are your favorites? Why? What do they have in common? What makes each so special?

Let's Find Out

1. It's about time to form your "clock" team of 4-6 players. Pick a familiar clock or make up your fantastic variation.
2. Make the team clock. You will need a framework, second hand, and minute hand. You can make such things as a bird for a cuckoo clock, a mouse for "Hickory Dickory Dock," and so on.
3. Make sure your clock runs smoothly.

Solve the Problem

What kinds of sounds did you make as your clock? Did you work together to make the sounds and movements? If you didn't quite do so to your satisfaction, why not try it again?

Follow-up Activities

• Conduct a "Clock Around the World" contest. Try making Big Ben, Grandfather Clocks, Swiss Clocks, and so on.
• Write a poem or short story about a clock.
• Make up a skit showing a human clock having a breakdown and fix it. Human and/or animal characters can be in the skit.

Become A Door

Think About It

Look at a door on the facing page. Discuss: What do doors do? Pick *one* example of how someone coming through a door made you feel special. Share the feelings. What would a door say if it could share *its* feelings?

Let's Find Out

1. Work in teams of four.
2. Two players become a door. One player will go through the door, and the other will greet him or her. Make sure the door is right for the place (for example, office room, palace, theatre).

Solve the Problem

What did the two people say to each other? If the door could speak, what would it say *after* the people left? Try it out.

Follow-up Activities

• Write a short paragraph, story, or poem describing the *secrets* a door might tell.
• Draw these stick figures in your notebook:

Then write a dialogue between the two characters. Share your scene.

Become An Elephant

Think About It

How much do you weigh? Did you know that an elephant can weigh 6,000 pounds? That's a *fact*. How would it *feel* if you were an elephant?

Let's Find Out

1. You'll need some help to become this one. Form a team of 6-8 players.
2. Two players form the elephant's body; two make the trunk; two, the tusks; and another two, the tail. Hello, elephant!

Solve the Problem

Still in the team as the elephant, tell how it feels to be so big and powerful. What happens when you move around a bit—describe your jungle environment.

Follow-up Activities

- Act out the delightful poem, "The Blind Man and the Elephant" by John Saxe.
- Work together and become other favorite animals in their natural environments. Draw some pictures of them.
- Discuss what people can do to protect endangered species, such as turtles and whales. How can we keep our environment clean and safe?

Become A Fountain

Think About It

Talk about the different kinds of fountains you've seen. What places do the fountains on the facing page make you think of? Imagine that the temperature is rising and you can cool off as a very friendly fountain. Describe how you feel.

Let's Find Out

1. Work together in teams of 6-8 players.
2. Discuss what kind of fountain you can become. Let your ideas flow—just like a fountain.
3. Create a fountain in majestic slow motion. Make sure you use levels with varying body positions.

Solve the Problem

What kind of fountain did you create? Give it a name, such as "Fountain of Youth," "Changing Colors," or a "Soda Fountain." What happens when soft, harmonious sounds are added to the fountain?

Follow-up Activities

• Using colored bits of paper, create a fountain collage with a partner or in a team.
• Do some research on famous fountains around the world. What is so special about each one?

Become A Garden

Think About It

Look at the flowers on the facing page. Let's create a garden right on-the-spot! Think about the *particular* flower you would like to be and why you like it so much. How would you feel among other flowers?

Let's Find Out

1. Imagine you are a tiny seed in the ground. Find a comfortable spot and curl up.
2. The sun is shining. Feel its warm glow on your seed body. Now it's raining...a gentle rain.
3. You are beginning to grow, ever so slowly. Feel your sides enlarge. Stretch your arms and fingers. What are you growing into? A yellow dandelion? A golden marigold? A pink rose? Or what?
4. Reach for the sky. Reach for the sun. There's a wind, a gentle breeze. Move in place as your flower. The sun is peeking out from behind a cloud. Fill your flower-body with its wonderful warmth.

Solve the Problem

Talk to each other as your flower. Say hello. Tell how you feel during a rainstorm and when the sun is out. Talk about the changes.

Follow-up Activities

• Become plants and trees in your garden. Add lively music, e.g., "Waltz of the Flowers" from *The Nutcracker Suite*.
• Talk about flowers, plants and trees. Why are they important?
• Draw or paint a garden scene. You also can use colored crepe paper or colored straws.

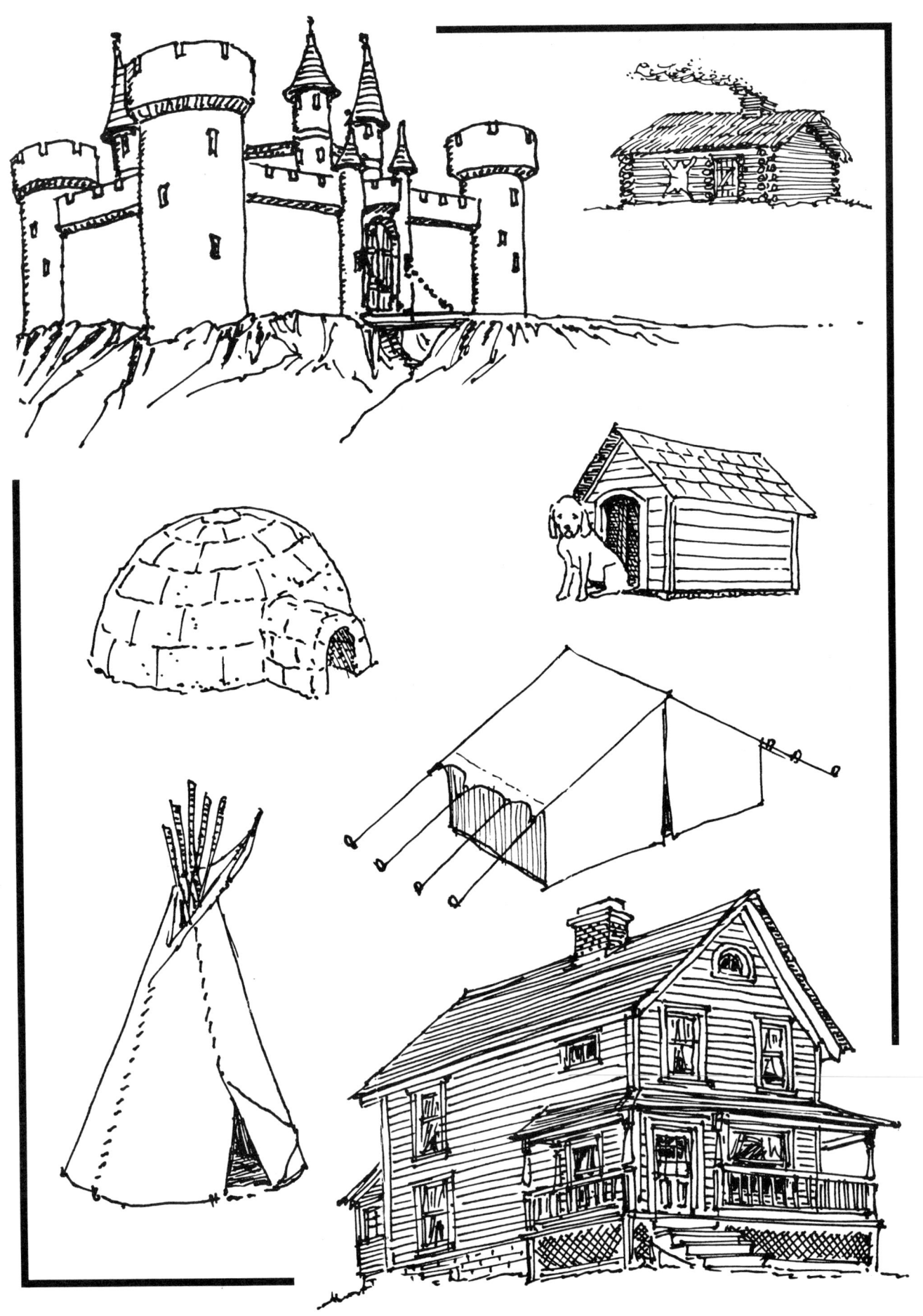

Become A House

Think About It

Look at the variety of houses on the facing page. How would you feel living in a palace or pagoda? How do you think houses feel about the people who occupy *them*?

Let's Find Out

1. Pick *one* of the houses on the facing page and form a team of players to become it.
2. Depending on the size of the house—and the size of your team—create either the whole house or just a part of it.
3. Make sure the parts of the house you show are connected correctly.

Solve the Problem

After you have made the house—or part of it—the team can discuss who would live in such a house. Who are these people? What do they say? What do they do? Now become the house again and gossip about the people who live in you.

Follow-up Activities

- Draw or paint the house you just made or create one from your imagination.
- Construct a house with wooden blocks. Expand the project—make a neighborhood or entire community. Give it a name, and tell how it would be run.

Become An Imaginary Object Or Person

| **Think About It** |

Brainstorm with your team the most fantastic, strangest, weirdest *imaginary* object or person you can think of. What is it, and what does it do? What is it called?

| **Let's Find Out** |

1. Experiment. Experiment. Experiment. (For example you might wish to *combine* objects and people.)
2. After you've come up with your fantastic imaginary object or person, give it a name.
3. Show it off—with pride.

| **Solve the Problem** |

What did you call your object or person? Why? How would you illustrate it?

| **Follow-up Activities** |

• Write a fantastic, strange, weird story about your imaginary object or person. Let your imagination run wild.
• Would you like to make any changes in your imaginary objects and/or people? What changes? Why?

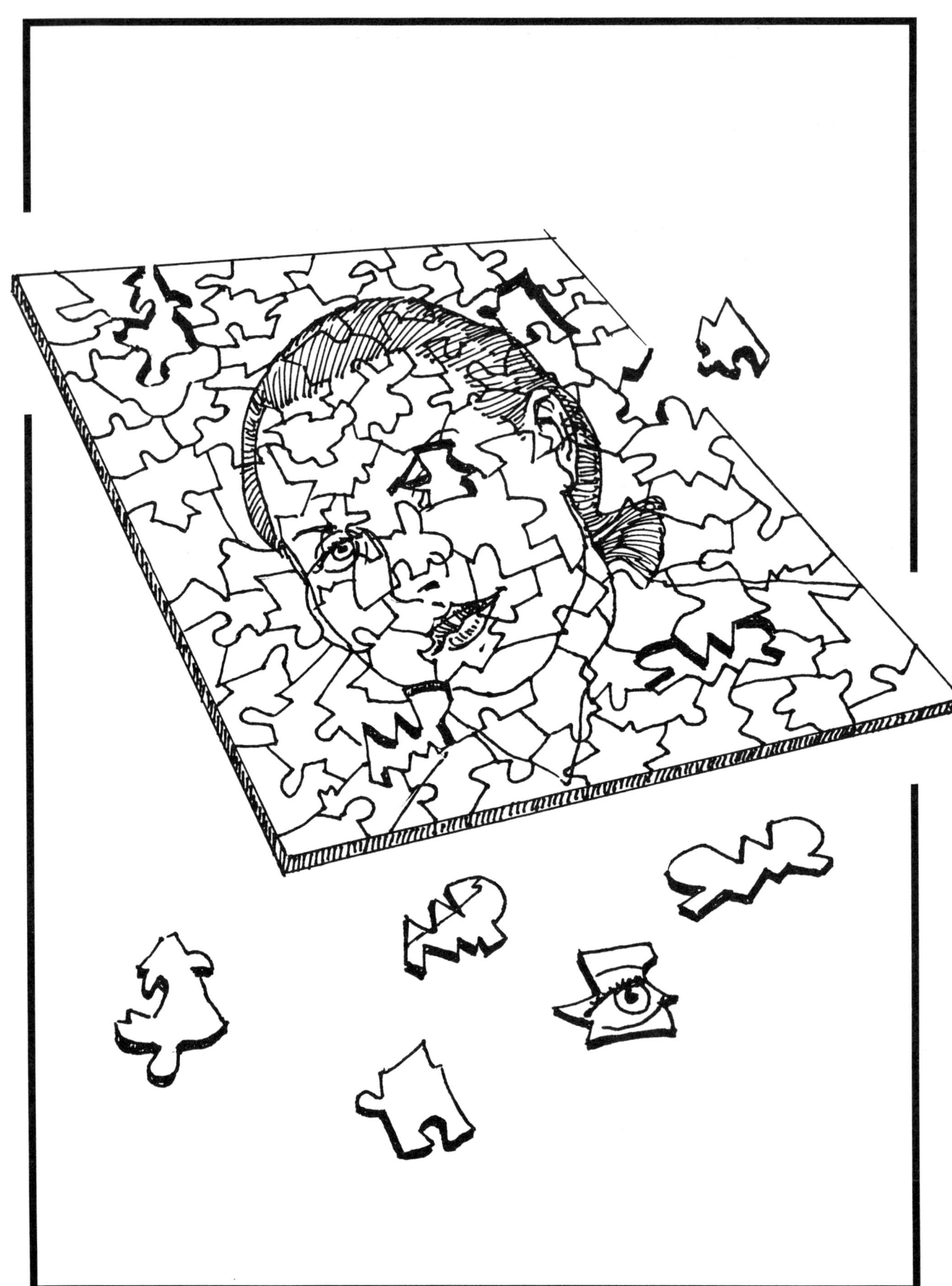

Become A Jigsaw Puzzle

Think About It

Look at the scrambled parts of a jigsaw puzzle on the facing page. You can put the picture easily together in your head. How would it feel if *you* were a piece of a puzzle waiting to be put together with the rest of the pieces?

Let's Find Out

1. Form two teams of 5-6 players each.
2. Each team gets together and quickly makes a familiar scene in pantomime, e.g., a sports scene, a winter scene, a school scene.
3. Now the players slowly break off from each other and scramble the parts of the scene—*each one still holding his or her original shape.*
4. It is the job of the players in the other team to correctly put the pieces back together.

Solve the Problem

While the players are in their unscrambled positions, they can tell how they feel being separated from the other pieces. These verbal clues can help the guessers correctly reassemble the parts.

Follow-up Activities

• Discuss what the exercise showed you about working together to solve the problems.
• Make a jigsaw puzzle from cardboard. How does it compare with the human jigsaw you made?

Become A Kitchen Appliance Or Utensil

Think About It

Look at the different things on the facing page that belong in a kitchen. What would you do or say if *you* were one of them?

Let's Find Out

1. Choose *one* of the things that belongs in a kitchen. Decide if you will show just the frame or the inside, or both. (For example, you might become the outline of a refrigerator with opening door or its inside compartments as well.)
2. When you have figured out how to make the object, discuss where it will be located in relationship to the other kitchen objects.

Solve the Problem

When you are standing in place as your object, tell what you do. You may even wish to brag a bit. Hold a meeting with the other appliances and offer your compliments and/or complaints. Are you used too much, or too little, not taken care of properly, or what?

Follow-up Activities

- Write a poem about one of the objects.
- Prepare a menu of some of your favorite foods and discuss how kitchen appliances and/or utensils are used in the preparation.

ABCDEFGHI *Play act* JKLMNOPQR STUVWXYZ

Become A Letter Of The Alphabet

Think About It

Do letters of the alphabet have feelings? Are t's crossed, i's strong, s's slithery? If you were an alphabet letter, how would *you* feel?

Let's Find Out

1. Make individual letters with your body. As the letters, tell how you feel.
2. Work with another player and make some more letters.
3. As a team, put some letters together and make a word.

Solve the Problem

What words did you make? Can you change the letters to form new words? As the letter, tell how you felt when you made the different words.

Follow-up Activities

• Experiment with small and capital letters.
• Scramble "living letters" of short words, e.g., rilg (girl). The teams must guess and physically rearrange the living letters.
• Become words used in a foreign language.

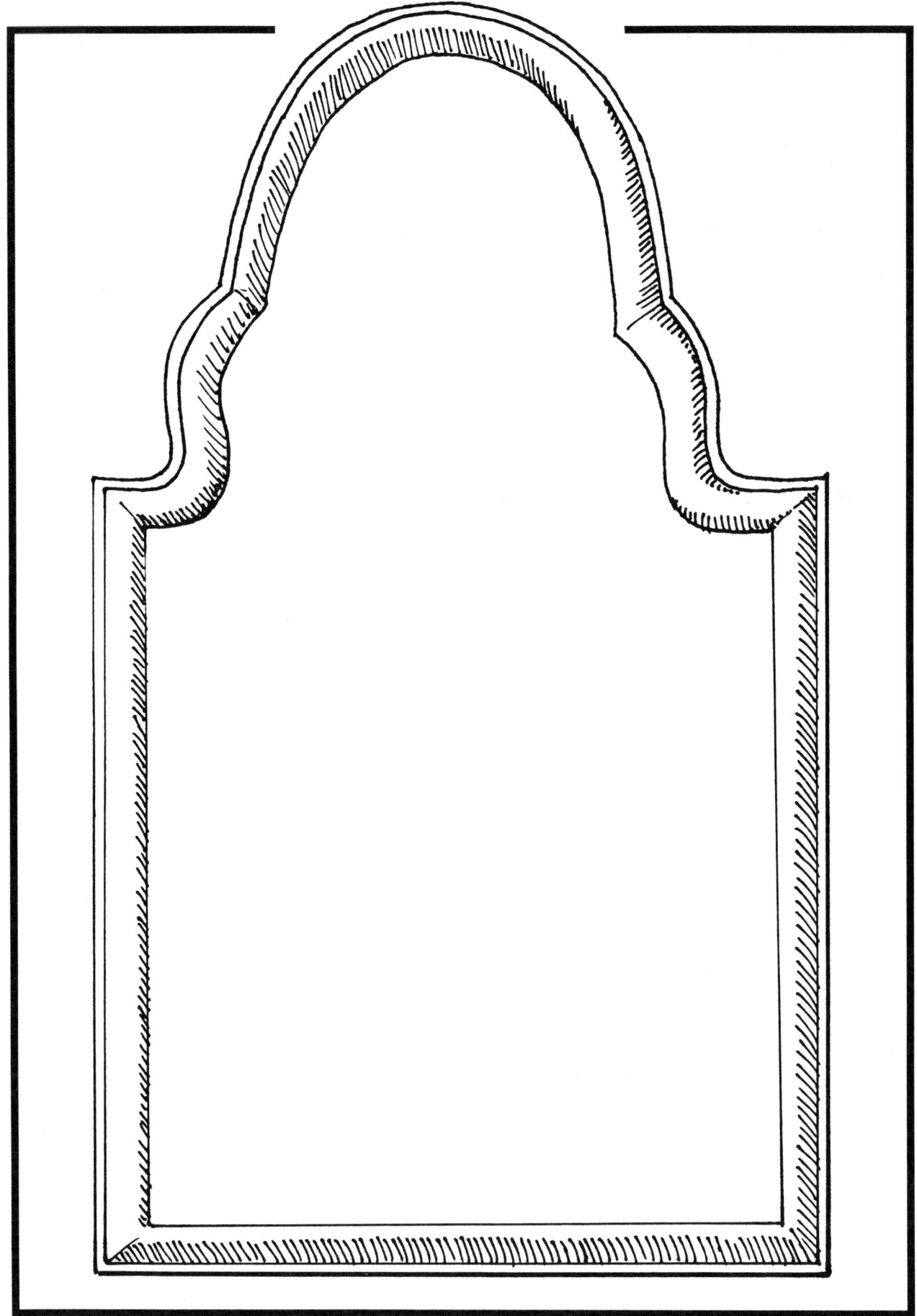

Become A Mirror

Think About It

Why do people use mirrors? Where do you find mirrors? Is it possible for people to mirror each other?

Let's Find Out

1. Work with a partner. One of you be A and the other B.
2. Both of you look into each other's eyes. Player A s-l-o-w-l-y moves his or her head and Player B copies as closely as possible.
3. Then Player B starts a slow movement of head and arms, and Player A copies exactly.
4. Now both players take turns following each other's head, arms, and body movements. You are a mirror!

Solve the Problem

Can you *move* as a mirror? You can if you go slow, keep eye contact, start with in-place movements, and then move around together in small areas.

Follow-up Activities

- As mirrors, perform familiar activities such as combing hair, playing sports in slow-mo, becoming seeds, and growing into trees and flowers.
- Talk about how it feels to be a mirror. If a mirror could talk, what would it say about you and your friends? Give an example.
- Draw "Mirror-People."

CHRISTOPHER

Karen

Barbara

Tony

Robert

William

Janet

WENDY

Lisa

Susan

Carlos

Michael

CLARK

Martin

Tanya

Thomas

Sharon

Andrew

Patricia

SAMANTHA

Become (Your) Name

Think About It

What's in a name? Do you know what your name means?
Mine, Milton, for example, means a mill town. Have you
ever thought about becoming your name?

Let's Find Out

1. Begin by writing your name in space, first using one arm
as a brush, then both arms, then your whole body.

2. Team up with a partner and work together to write or
print each other's name in space. Add a dash of color—or
some soft sounds.

3. Act out some of your names. For example, for Milton, a
mill town, the player could be a flour mill. For Jonah, which
means dove, there could be a gentle flying movement. For
Beth, which means house, 2 or 3 players could form a tent.

Solve the Problem

How did it feel writing or printing your name in space?
What did you learn about each other's names when you
enacted them?

Follow-up Activities

• Look up the meanings of names in a dictionary. Share your
  discoveries.
• Write a poem entitled "The Name Game."
• Draw a name acrostic for your name or the name of a
  friend.

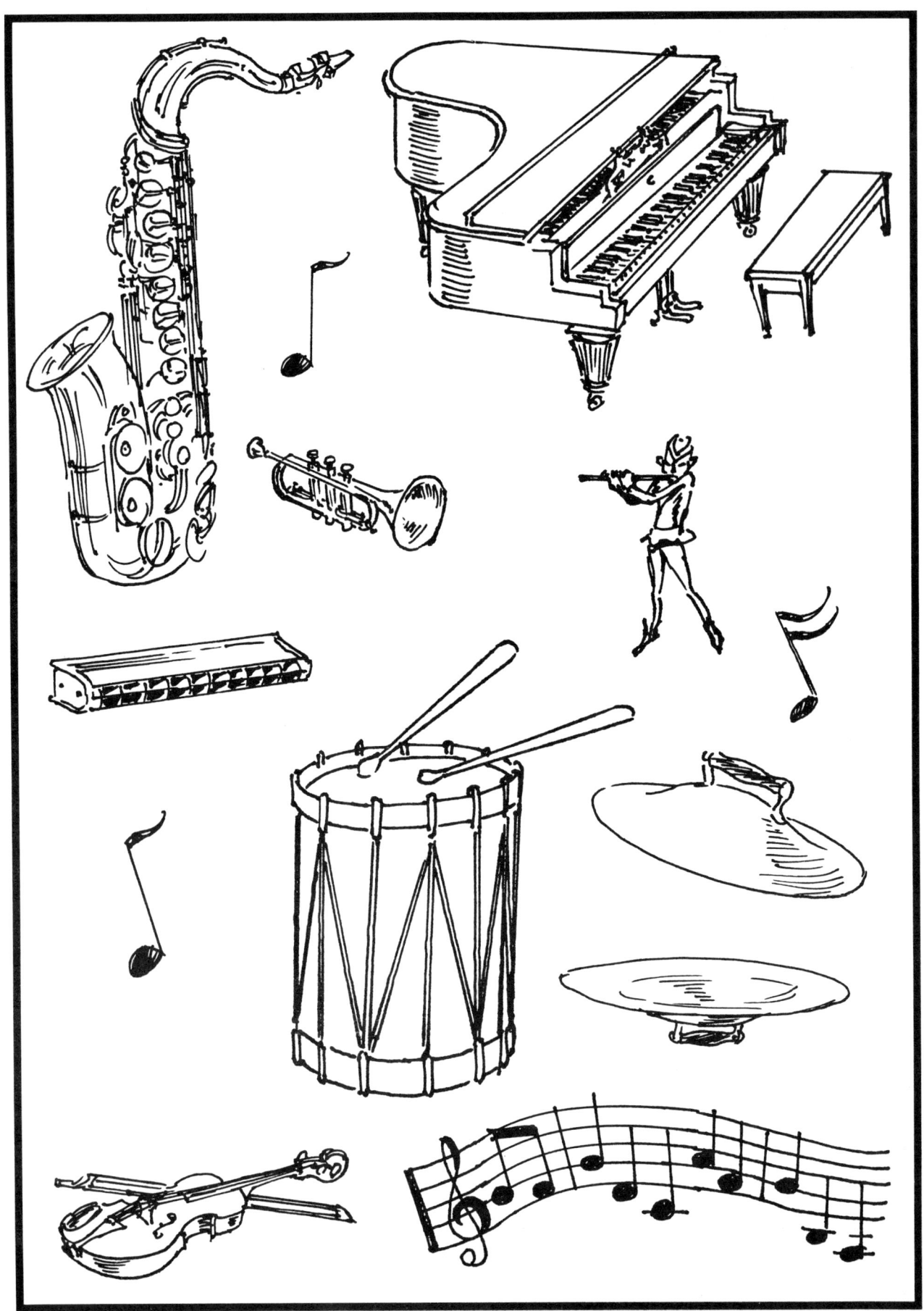

Become An Orchestra

Think About It

Look at the different musical instruments on the facing page. They all belong in an orchestra. What kinds of sounds do they make? How could you *become* some of the instruments?

Let's Find Out

1. As a warm-up, for a few minutes, pantomime playing one of the instruments. Then add sounds.
2. Choose one of the instruments and, with a partner, become it. For example, one pair could become a piano swaying back and forth with a double row of black and white keys. Another person on your team could play the piano.
3. Choose a conductor to lead the human orchestra.

Solve the Problem

Can you work together to play an *entire* song? Keep on trying until you are all playing in harmony!

Follow-up Activities

- Play some more familiar songs. Choose some more conductors.
- Make up an original song that everyone can play together.
- Try some silhouette poses behind a lighted screen.

Become A Painting

Think About It

Look at the painting on the facing page. What do you like about them? Why? Pick *one* of the paintings. What if you could make it come alive?

Let's Find Out

1. Form a team to act out one of the paintings on the facing page or choose another painting from a book or magazine.
2. Players can become the objects and/or people in the painting. No one say a word. Then after a minute or so, let the scene come alive.

Solve the Problem

Think about what each player on the team will say as the person or object. Make sure each player speaks one at a time.

Follow-up Activities

- If the painting does not have a title, why not give it one now?
- Rearrange the people and/or objects in the painting.
- Make your own colorful painting and act it out.

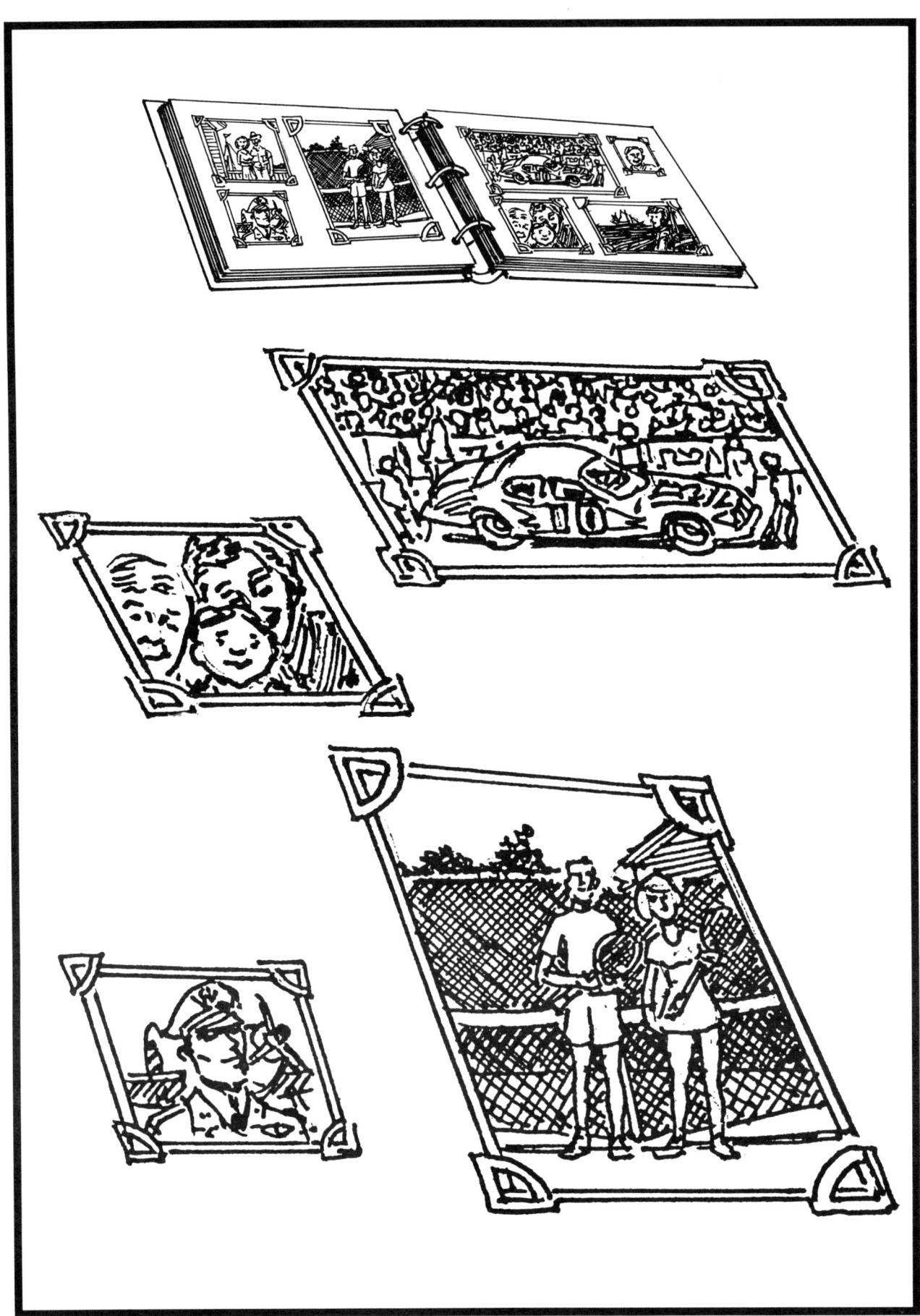

Become A Photo Album

Think About It

Now, how would you like to become three connected parts of a *very* short story? Think of an exciting moment from your life that you would be happy to include in a photo album.

Let's Find Out

1. Work with a team of 4-5 players. Share your exciting moments and decide which one to do.
2. Decide on three snapshots that will be *frozen* in time. For example: a basketball player is surrounded by the rest of the team. Click! Second snapshot: a basketball player shoots the ball into a human hoop. Third snapshot: the referee signals the basket counts.
3. Make sure that in each of the three snapshots the final second is *frozen* —no movement. The composition is supposed to look like a still photo.

Solve the Problem

How did it feel being the people and things in the photos? If the people in the photos could speak, what would they say? What other events might you include in your photo album to tell a *very* short story?

Follow-up Activities

- Share some of your photos with your friends.
- What if you could write a caption (a short sentence or pharse describing a picture) for some of the photos? What would you write? Why?

SHHHHHHH!

Become A Quiet...

Think About It

Think of some scenes in life that are very, very quiet—such as snow falling on a tree or the sun slowly setting behind a mountain. You could become a quiet scene with your teammates using only your imaginations and bodies.

Let's Find Out

1. Discuss a possible quiet scene to create with your team.
2. Plan *who* and *what* will be in the scene. *Where* will it take place? How many players will be needed? What will the players be *doing*?
3. Present the scene—no talking, please.

Solve the Problem

How did the scene go? Was it as quiet as possible? If not, what can you do to make the scene work even better? Try it.

Follow-up Activities

• Draw the scene you made up or create another one.
• Write a poem entitled "Quiet."

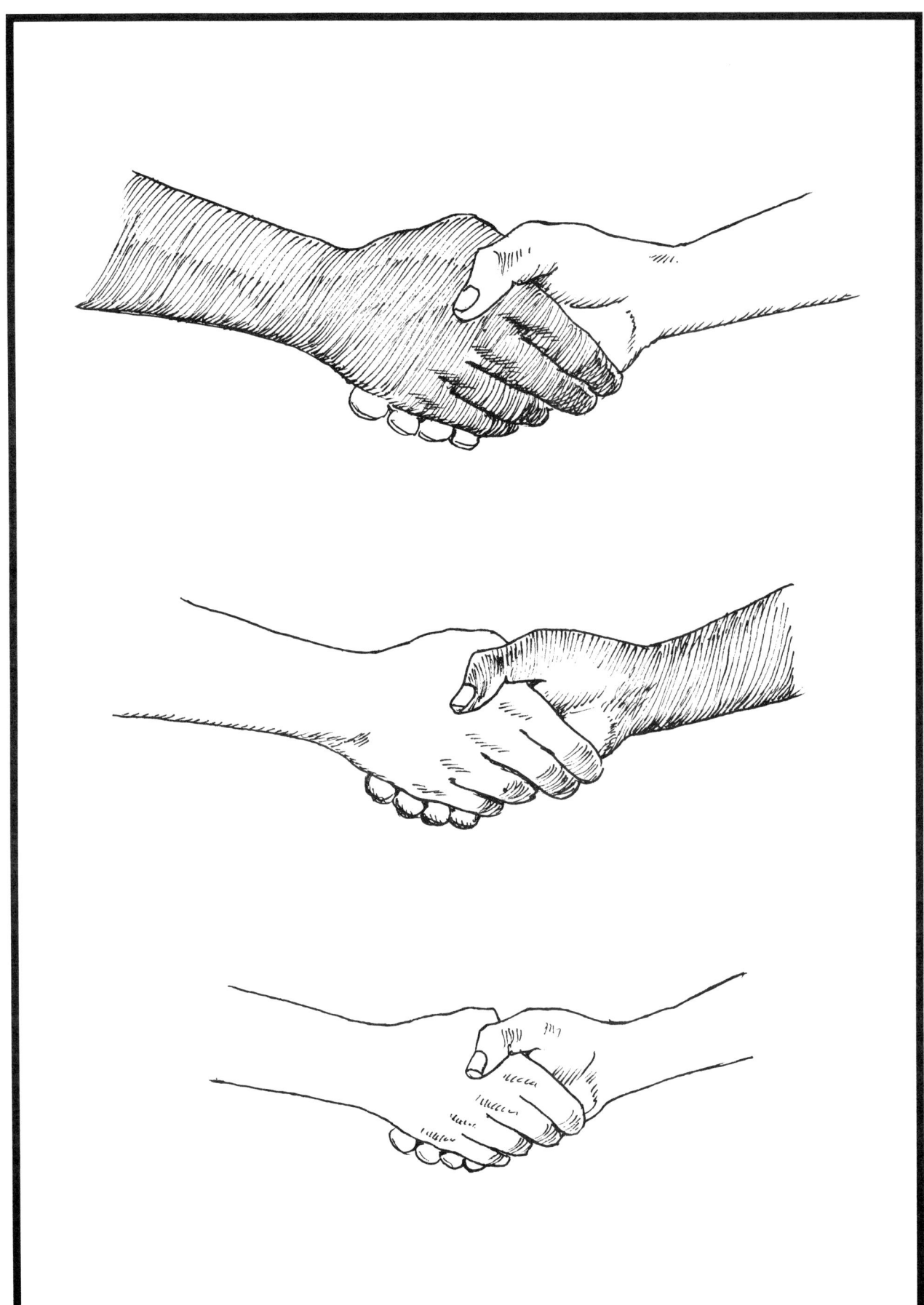

Become The Quintessence Of...

Think About It

Wouldn't it be wonderful if you could describe the *very* essence—the heart—of something positive in its most con-centrated form? What, for example, is the quintessence of friendship, of peace, of harmony, of...

Let's Find Out

1. With your team, pick a positive theme or concept that brings people together, such as friendship.
2. Work together and create a team sculpture showing the quintessence of the concept.
3. Present your creation perhaps as a still photo, painting, or ad.

Solve the Problem

What if your creation could come alive? What kinds of sounds would you make? Show us. Experiment with some more variations on the theme and share your results.

Follow-up Activities

• Draw your own version of the team creation.
• Work with a partner, and write a story or song about the experience.

Become A River

Think About It

Why are rivers important? What are some of the things rivers can do that are helpful and harmful? How do you think a river would feel if it were polluted?

Let's Find Out

1. Form two teams of 6-8 players each. Each team forms a river.
2. One team enacts a scene in which the river is *helpful*, the other, *harmful*. Discuss the situations, and then switch the teams so they can experience the other situation.
3. Now one of the rivers flows along as the other team becomes pollutants (chemicals, oil, garbage, medical waste, and so on) contaminating the river. Discuss and switch teams.

Solve the Problem

How did your river feel when it was in a *helpful* situation? When it was in a *harmful* situation? What did the river do when it was polluted? How did you show this? What kinds of movements and sounds did you use?

Follow-up Activities

• Form a panel to discuss what people can do to prevent the pollution of precious rivers, streams, oceans and lakes.
• Write and illustrate a poem called "Rivers."

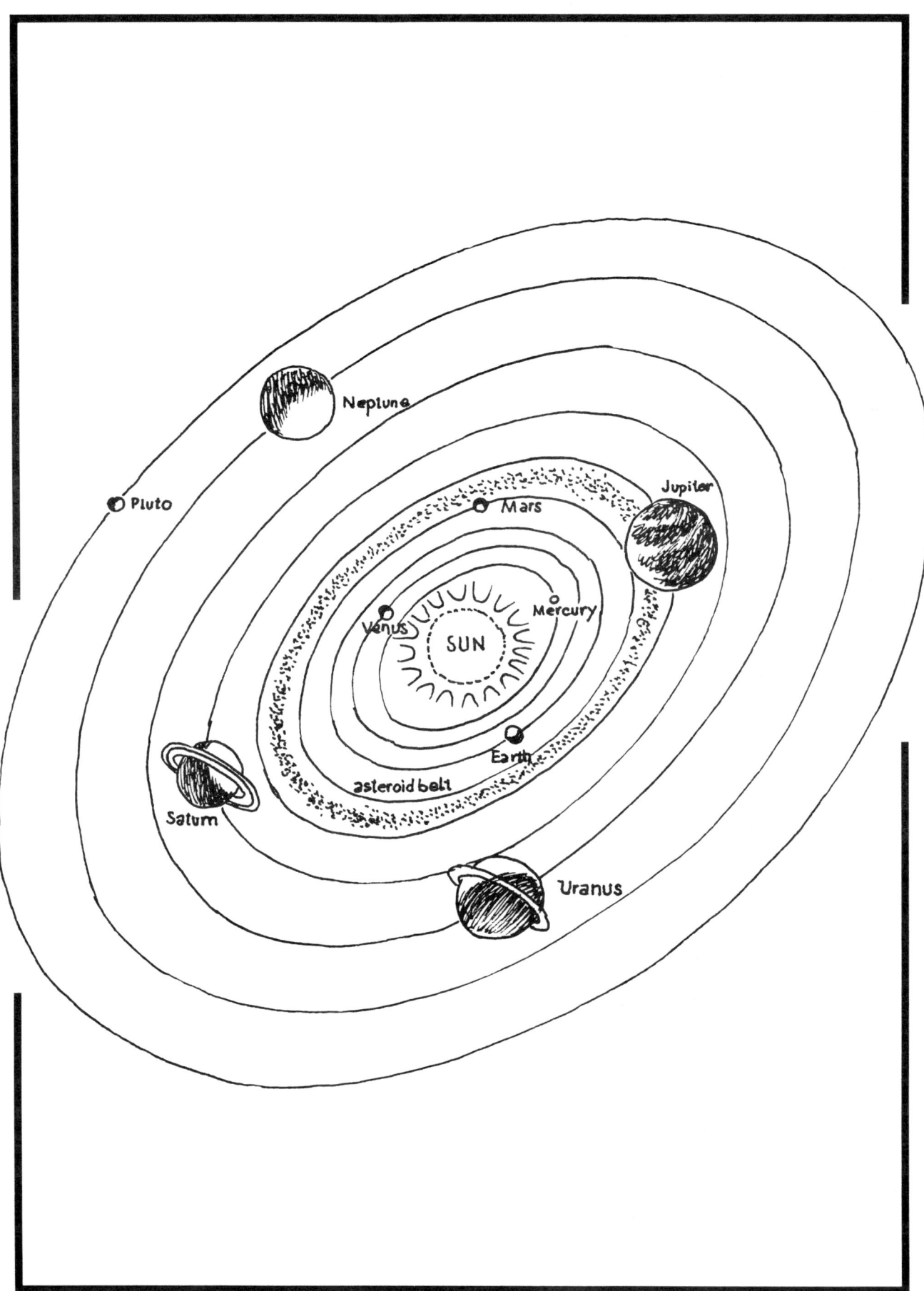

Become A Solar System

Think About It

What if you could take a spaceship and visit other planets in our galaxy? What if you could become some of the planets in our solar system? What would you do? How would you feel?

Let's Find Out

1. Look at the chart on the facing page. It shows our solar system.
2. In your team (8-10 players), plan how you will show the solar system with your bodies. For example, Mercury, the smallest planet, is nearest to the sun. With two players as Mercury, one side could face the sun and be bright and hot; the other side, always cold and dark. How could this be shown? How can you make Jupiter's moons, Saturn's rings, and so on? First, you may have to check out the facts.
3. Experiment. Enjoy. Elaborate.

Solve the Problem

While assuming your position in the solar system, tell a *fact* or two about your planet. Also tell how you feel—powerful, small, lively, unusual, and so on.

Follow-up Activities

• Draw your own version of the solar system.
• Write a short story or poem about it.
• Make up a science sequence showing the sun in the center and the other planets revolving on a chalked orbit at different speeds. Use "astral" music as they orbit the sun.

Become A Sound/Motion Machine

Think About It

What is a machine? What do machines do? Not all machines make things. Some are just for fun. For example, can you make a machine that connects sounds and motions?

Let's Find Out

1. Work together in a team of 4-6 players.
2. Player #1 makes a soft sound and slow movement of arms. Repeat this sound and movement over and over in harmony and with style.
3. Player #2 connects to the first player with a new sound and movement that blends with the first player's sound and movement.
4. The rest of the players each join in connecting the sounds and movements until the machine is running smoothly.
5. Make sure different levels of bodies and contrasting sounds are used. The sound and movement should flow in harmony.

Solve the Problem

Discuss how the different parts of the machine were related and why the machine ran smoothly. Are there any ways the machine could be improved? Try them out!

Follow-up Activities

- Make a machine that shows a concept or process studied in science such as a photosynthesis machine.
- Create a time machine and go back in time or into the future for some interviews.
- Become robots, "walking," "eating," "talking," "working," "playing" mechanically.

Become A Television Set

Think About It

In a team, talk about some of your favorite television programs. Why do you like them? What kinds of programs would you like to see on TV?

Let's Find Out

1. Two players form the TV's square box.
2. Another player, with arms straight up, becomes the TV antenna.
3. You now have a basic TV set!

Solve the Problem

You still have to see your favorite television shows. Easy. A team of 2-3 players can take turns acting bits of TV shows—science fiction, comedy, news programs—inside the TV frame, while a viewer in front of the "set" switches its channels from time to time.

Follow-up Activities

• How can you show a TV program that is in color?
• Make up some commercials or scenes from movies that can be presented.

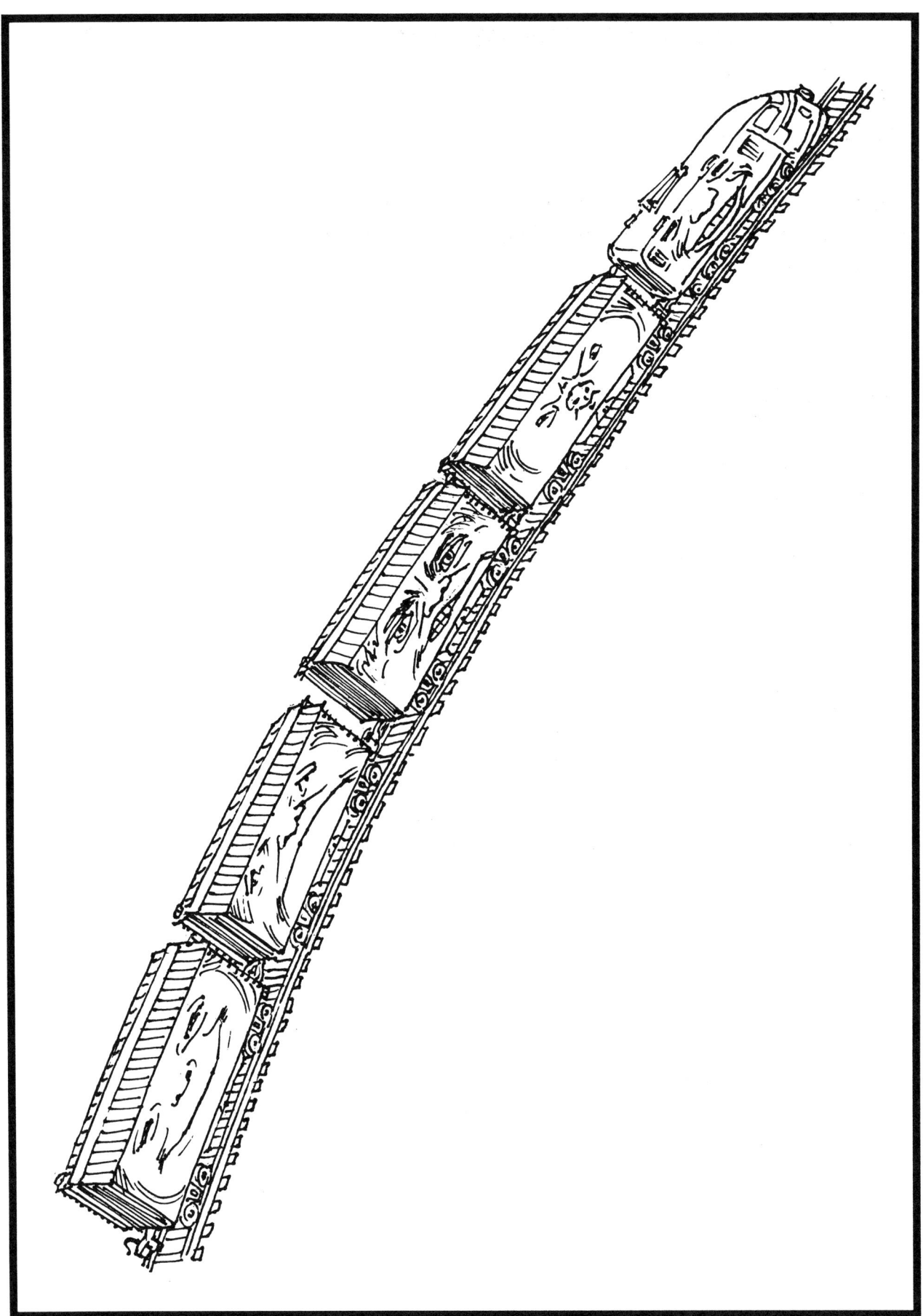

Become A Train Of Moods

Think About It

What is a mood? Name some different moods you have experienced. What do you think caused these moods? Can you create different moods?

Let's Find Out

1. Form a long line, 6-8 players, each one holding the waist of the player in front.
2. The player at the front of the line can now call out a mood, such as happy, sad, or angry.
3. Now the players can put the train—living chain—in gear and capture the mood through combinations of sound and movement.
4. After a few minutes, the player at the head of the train goes to the end of the line. The next player can call out a new word.

Solve the Problem

What moods did you become? How did it feel making them up? How did it feel working together to make them up?

Follow-up Activities

- Design an artistic collage of moods.
- Write a short poem called "Moods."
- Use a few different "mood" music selections—e.g., blues, scary, military, lazy-drowsy, nervous, etc. Others can guess which is acted out.

Become An Umbrella

Think About It

Oh, the sun will come out tomorrow. But what if it rains instead? You will need an umbrella. Can your team become one on-the-spot? What will it do?

Let's Find Out

1. Get together with your team of 5-6 players and figure out a way to make a giant umbrella.
2. Plan this: Who will be the umbrella stick? Who will be the spokes? How will the cloth be shown?

Solve the Problem

Now that you are an umbrella, what can you do? Some players can portray diverse weather conditions the umbrella reacts to. How does the umbrella react to a mild rain pour, to a harsh gale or a hurricane? Show the reactions in slow motion. Players can make appropriate sounds as both the umbrella and as the different weather conditions.

Follow-up Activities

• Draw a BIG umbrella for display on the wall. Let yourself go when it comes to color and design!
• Make up a team story about an umbrella that gets blown around the world.

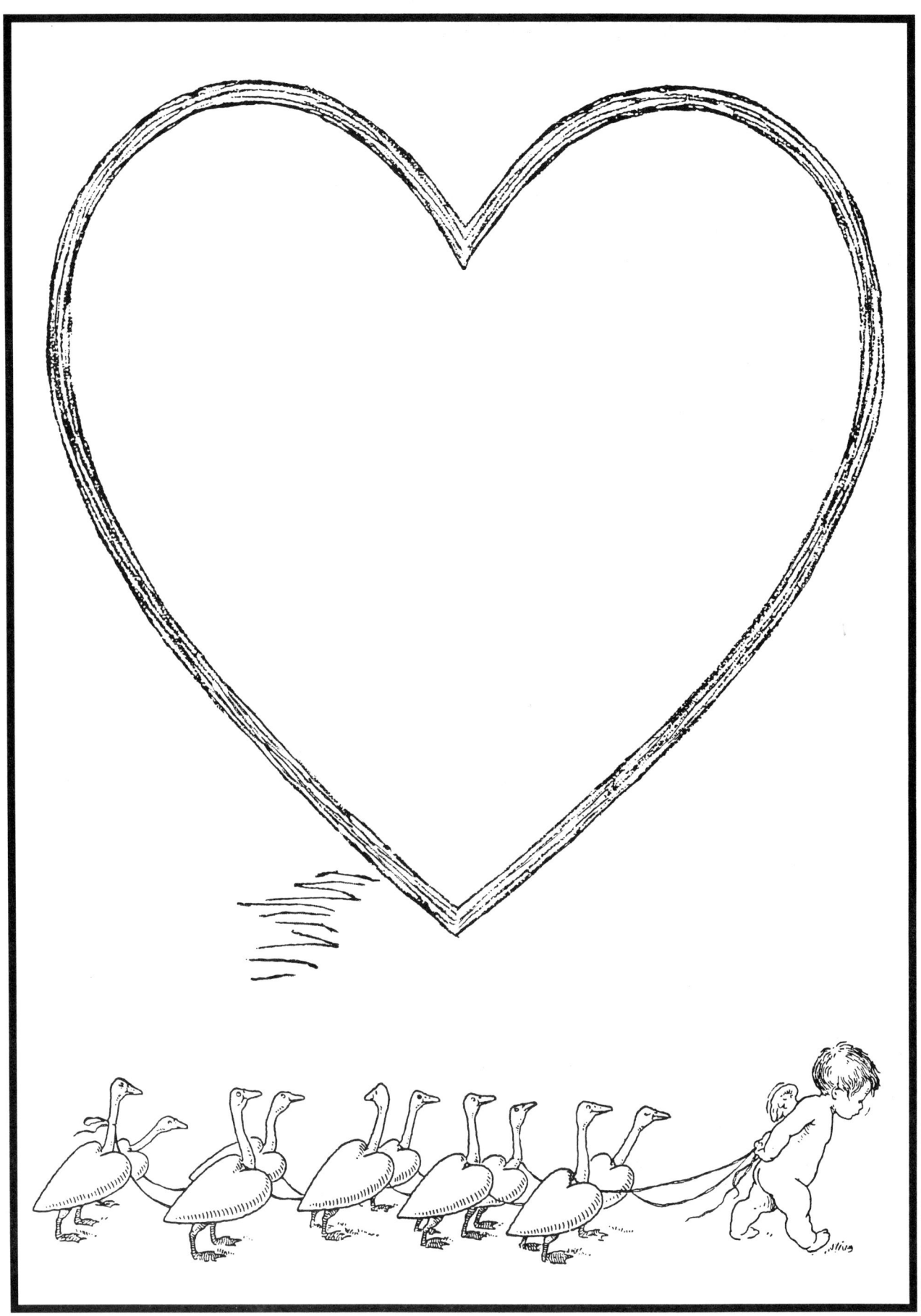

Become A Valentine

Think About It

It's fun to buy a valentine, more fun to make one, and perhaps the most fun to actually become one. So even though it may not be Saint Valentine's Day today, can we get into the friendly holiday spirit?

Let's Find Out

1. Form a circle with a team of 6-8 players. Everyone joins hands.
2. Now slowly make the shape of a big heart.
3. Like the pulsing of a heart, players move toward the center and back again, back and forth, back and forth, holding hands and following the heartbeat. Add some sounds.
4. You now are a living, pulsating, rhythmical heart.

Solve the Problem

How did you capture the spirit of friendship when you made the team heart? What did you like best about becoming the valentine?

Follow-up Activities

• Write a friendly poem about creating the valentine.
• Repeat the exercise. This time sing a song while in the heart formation.
• Repeat the exercise and play music that fits the scene.

Become A Whale

Think About It

Look at the picture on the facing page of the whale. Did you know that the whale is the largest animal in the world? Some whales, called "Blue Whales" can reach 100 feet long! That's a fact. How would you feel if you were a whale that big?

Let's Find Out

1. You'll need as many players as possible to make the length of the whale.
2. Each player holds the waist of the player in front. Everyone then levels off to form the shape of the whale. Several players will be needed to become the whale's fluke and flippers.

Solve the Problem

Can you get your whale to move around the space, pretending that it's under water? After the whale has slowly moved around a bit, the players can break off from a circle, and take turns explaining how the whale breathes and eats its food and other interesting things. If more research is needed, players can pick up the discussion at a later time.

Follow-up Activities

• Write a song about "Big Blue."
• Draw a picture or write a story about other endangered species of the sea kingdom, e.g., turtles and dolphins.

Become A Xylophone

Think About It

Look at the pictures of the xylophones on the facing page. They vary from having 8 to 44 metal bars. The tones they produce are something special. Discuss what kinds of sounds they make. If you were a xylophone, which song would you play?

Let's Find Out

1. Form a horizontal line.
2. Everyone in the team of 8 players stretches his or her right hand out, palm up.
3. Figure out the eight note scale.
4. Designate the xylophone player(s) who lightly touch(es) the palm of the players to produce the sounds.
5. Have fun! Play a song!

Solve the Problem

How did the song turn out? Do your efforts possibly need more work? Then work on the song some more.

Follow-up Activities

• Try out some other songs. Change the xylophone players from time to time.
• Work together and write an original song. Give it a title. Make up some words for your song.

Become The Mysterious "X"

Think About It

There are only two pages or so of X's in the dictionary. That means there are not many objects starting with X to choose from. Can you do it?

Let's Find Out

Reach for that dictionary and look for those nouns. If you decide to become a copy machine, remember *Xerox* is a trade name, so give the company credit if you write about becoming one of its copiers.

Solve the Problem

Did you find the X word? If not, keep on trying.

Follow-up Activities

- After you have made your mysterious X object, figure out some fun activities you can follow up with.
- Now think of words that sound like X (i.e., "ex"): *Excuse me! express, extra.* How many can you think of? Share your *ex*amples

Ha-Ha

Ha-Ha

Ha-Ha

Ha-Ha

Ha-Ha

Ha-Ha

Ha-Ha

Ha-Ha

HA-HA

Ha-H

Ha-Ha

Become A "Yarn"

| Think About It |

No, this is not the kind of yarn you knit with. You've already become a ball of yarn (page 13). Yarn here means a funny story. Choose a joke, riddle or story that has at least one inanimate object or an animal in it. For example: Why is someone who sings a long time like a pony? Answer: They're both a little hoarse. How can you make your joke come alive?

| Let's Find Out |

1. As usual, work in your team to figure out how you can become the object. You may need human characters, too.
2. Act out the yarn. Dialogue can be used in the skit. For instance, in the hoarse example, a singer might talk to his or her audience. The horse could talk, too.

| Solve the Problem |

Was your presentation funny? Did it have a lot of yucks? We hope so!

| Follow-up Activities |

• Act out some more yarns, perhaps something funny that happened to you.

Become A Zoological Garden (Zoo)

Think About It

You've already become a garden of flowers. Now here's your chance to become some of your favorite animals or birds in a zoological garden. Pick your animal or bird right now. Where will you be in the zoo?

Let's Find Out

1. Everyone share what animal or bird you will be.
2. Together, plan the layout of the zoo.
3. Become the animals and birds using pantomime, sounds, and music.
4. All creatures in the zoo: pose for a photograph.

Solve the Problem

What surprises did you experience in becoming the zoological garden? Do you think you will feel different when you visit a zoo next time? How so?

Follow-up Activities

- Choose some of the animals and birds you became and create a scene where they are in their natural habitat.
- Draw some pictures of animals and birds.

Notes

Part Two
~Creating With More Movement and Verbal Games~

MOVING ON...

Part Two shows how to make learning come alive for young people when they exercise their bodies, develop their senses, create opportunities for responsible social interaction, and tap their creativity potential. Five sections: "Let's Move!," "Say It in Silence," "Speak Up!" "Learning through Language," and "Let's Find Out" utilize a broad range of drama techniques including pantomiming , improvisation, body movement, and oral communication. The games can be used to expand on the content of any elementary school and middle school curriculum because they engage the child in activities that require problem solving, inquiry, recall, and other learning skills. The games are easily adaptable to meet individual classroom or group needs.

LET'S MOVE!

Now you can be anything, anyone—
Just move your body to start the fun!
Take giant steps across the land and sea,
Stretch your body to be as big as it can be...
Imagine you are a bird, a daisy;
Wiggle, bend and leap—don't be lazy!

Group gravity

Travel through imaginary worlds and overcome amazing obstacles! Children must concentrate and respond to suggestions made by the leader.

1. Whole class forms a circle.
2. One student (the teacher for primary grades) is the caller. This person says, "You are moving through molasses. It's thick and sticky." The caller has a drum or tambourine and beats a slow rhythm.
3. The caller must then say, "You are trying to hurry through the molasses. You are struggling... faster and faster." The caller speeds up the beat.
4. Caller may change the setting whenever desired.
5. Change the caller every few minutes.

Try This
• Walk on the moon (remember, there is less gravity there than on the Earth), or float in

outer space.
- Walk on different surfaces such as sand, mud, water, snow, ice, and rock.
- Vary the temperatures and combine them with different substances. For example, when you are walking through snow, the sun suddenly comes out, the weather warms up, and the snow begins to melt.

Change the place

Provides an opportunity for children to let their imaginations flow freely within a structured setting. Teacher directs children by making creative suggestions throughout the activity.

Preparation: Briefly talk about the different feelings associated with the changing seasons.

1. Circle formation.

2. Teacher announces, "Let's imagine that it's summer, and you have your bathing suit on. Everybody into the pool!" Children pantomime swimming and splashing within the confines of the circle.

3. Teacher announces that the pool is freezing over, and the pool becomes an ice-skating rink. Children are instructed to go to their lockers (perimeters of the circle) to change into warm, winter clothing and carefully put on their skates. Children pantomime skating, sliding, and pirouetting.

4. Now, teacher announces that it is getting dark out (someone can actually dim the classroom lights), and that plants are beginning to sprout from cracks in the ice. Slowly, trees and bushes continue growing until children find themselves in the middle of a tropical rainforest. Children silently transform into their favorite jungle animals or birds. They can pantomime hunting for food, playing, flying, or whatever. After awhile, the animals all go to sleep and slowly wake up as children.

5. Now they can write a story or poem, or perhaps draw a picture about the feelings they have just experienced.

Try This
• Extend the fantasy trip, so that the children slowly become astronauts, don space outfits, and float onto the moon's surface in slow-motion; or the children can explore foreign countries and magical kingdoms.

Move like me

Provides an opportunity for physical exercise, aids in physical coordination, and helps children express their feelings through movement. Note: This is a good game for both the schoolyard and the classroom.

1. Players form two teams facing each other at opposite sides of the room. A player from one side begins an action and moves toward the opposing team. He or she might clap, stamp, wiggle, or yodel while advancing.
2. When this player reaches the opposite side, he or she taps the player standing directly in front and they switch places. The tapped player then assumes the actions of the first player, and starts moving across the room.
3. The new player adds to and changes the actions while progressing toward the opposing team.
4. The steps are repeated and game continues.

Try This
• Pattern some movements after historical characters. Example: One child becomes Harriet Tubman moving silently through the night. The player tapped also mimes Tubman, but then changes to a Civil Rights marcher.
• Use the same game with sound repetition instead.
• Play different types of music during the game.

Ali gazanga

A marvelous ice-breaker! Develops concentration and coordination. Every one gets a chance to lead the group, and develop self-confidence. Great during recreation time or indoor line-up on a rainy day. Goes on and on and everyone loves it!

1. Children either stand by their desks or form a circle.
2. Leader calls out part of the chant while making a short, concise action with body—such as tossing hands into the air, shaking body, clapping hands, or hopping on one foot.
3. Children join chant and mimic the leader's movements.
4. The movements become more complicated as chant continues.
5. Ring a bell to freeze action. Choose a new leader and continue.

Try This

- Make up your own chant.
- Use the hallways as an alternate area.
- Have children illustrate *their* body movements or the ones they saw and liked best.
- Have a "make up your own chant" contest.
- Introduce a drum or tambourine for rhythm.

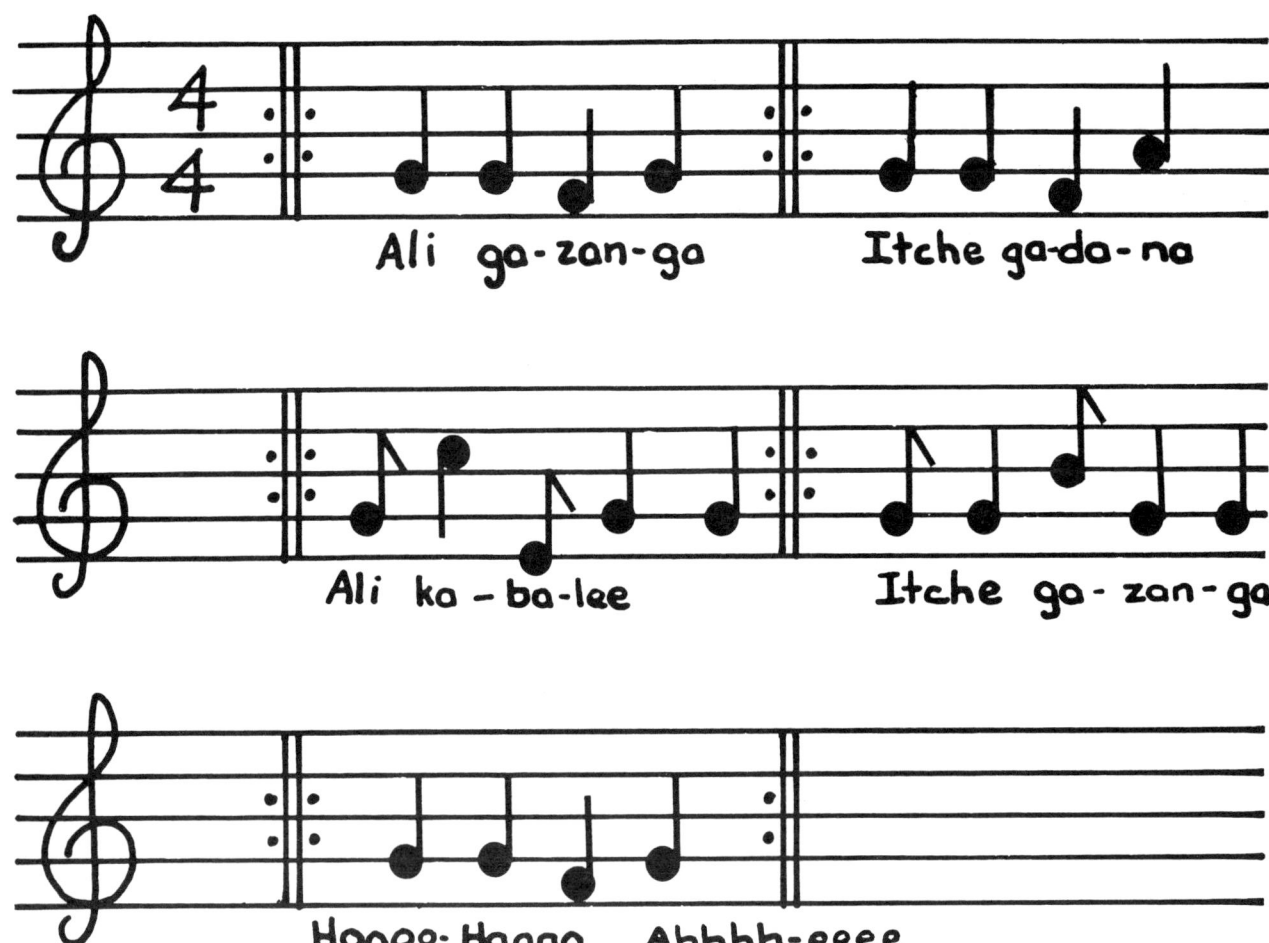

Be the thing

Children get a "feel" for how an object is constructed or works by actually becoming the object.

Preparation: Children look around the room and carefully observe the size, shape, and texture of various objects.

1. Divide the class into four groups.

2. Group 1 picks an object in the room for Group 2 to become as a whole (for example, a table); Group 3 picks a different object for Group 4 to become.

3. After the two groups have become the objects, the other two groups will then do something

with, to, or at the objects. For example, Group 1 can eat at Group 2's "table"; Group 3 can ride Group 4's "car."

Try This
• Become objects that are outside the classroom, such as a stove, a sofa, a stereo, or whatever.

Shoes are the clues!
What would you do if you could wear any shoe? Let's find out...

1. Tell children they will be taking a series of "Imagination Trips." They will pretend to be wearing different kinds of shoes on each trip.
2. Tap out a variety of rhythms on a drum or woodblock as children move quietly in tempo.
3. Change the beat periodically. Each time you change the beat, make an announcement: "You are wearing tennis shoes; show us how you would move on a tennis court." Help to create the mood by using vivid imagery:

"The sun is hot and you're in your tennis shorts. You can feel the warm concrete under your shoes. You feel nice and light as you bounce around. What are you holding? Show us in pantomime."

4. Change beat, continue instructions: "Now you're wearing heavy galoshes and you're knee-deep in snow. Show us how you would move in the galoshes. The snow is getting deeper!"
5. Change the kind of shoes frequently. Use ballet slippers (dancing), astronaut boots (floating), and so on.

Try This
• Use tools instead of shoes: a hammer (carpenter), a drill (construction worker), hair clippers (barber), and so on.

Microbes to monsters
Children experience the delight of going through a variety of creative changes involving the body and the mind.

Preparation: Explain that microbes are a tiny form of life, such as germs or bacteria.

1. Children lie down on the floor. Ask them to imagine that they are tiny, invisible microbes, which will soon grow into giants, plants, or monsters.
2. To the accompaniment of appropriate "creation" music (such as Holst's "The Planets"), the children start slowly and silently evolving into giant creatures. Have them stretch their giant bodies.
3. Now, children imagine finding a mountain of clay. They knead it and mold it into a giant object.
4. Children give their creations to a neighbor after pantomiming what it is.

5. Once again, children feel their bodies growing and expanding until they are so HUGE that they occupy the entire space of the room!

6. Children imagine that they are stepping from one planet to another as they take gigantic strides across the room.

7. Have children freeze. Slowly, they must make themselves as small as can be by curling up on the floor. Ask them to imagine that they are sleeping in a thimble or matchbox.

8. When they wake, children return to their places quietly.

9. Have children write stories about their experience. If time, let them illustrate the stories with bright colors.

SAY IT IN SILENCE

Silence brings thoughts and feelings, too:
What am I thinking when I smile at you?
What does it mean if I nod my head?
What would you do if I frowned instead?
How many things can I say without a word?
And will you understand, if you've watched, but not heard?

Change the object
A quiet game that helps to develop manual dexterity.

Preparation: Children mold from clay objects of their choice.

1. Have three or four groups form separate circles.

2. In each group, beginning player molds one imaginary object without talking (an animal, ball, jewelry, toy, clock) and then passes the object to the next player in the circle.

3. Player 2 takes the object, briefly does something with it to form another object, and passes it on.

4. Player 3 takes this object, briefly does something with it to make a new object, and passes it on. This continues until everyone in the circle has had a chance to change an object and to make a new one.

5. Encourage silence during this game, except when someone asks the object to be named if it is not clear. Hint: When making an object in silence, players should concentrate on its shape, size, weight, and texture.

Try This

• Have children write detailed descriptions of their clay sculptures.

• Make and change objects found in the kitchen, in school, in a particular historical period, or

from a particular country.
- Use snap-together building blocks instead of clay.
- Display clay sculptures.

Page to stage

Make the pages of a favorite story come alive! Children get the chance to show how they would act when placed in the situations of their favorite story characters.

1. Class chooses a favorite story or nursery rhyme.
2. Ask for volunteers to pantomime the basic actions of characters as you read all or part of the story. (You may want to stop the story at appropriate places and pick new volunteers.)

Try This
- Use other literary sources with older children. Sometimes they might add their own improvised theatrics. For example, Macbeth's dagger soliloquy can be turned into a comedy. A comic opera, such as *The Barber of Seville,* can be told as a story.
- Have the children share their ideas of how stories or nursery rhymes might otherwise end.

Japanese tea ceremony

A good game for teaching the customs of another country.

Preparation: Pair off players in a circle. In each pair, one player is HOST, and the other is GUEST. HOST and GUEST face each other in seated position on the floor, cross-legged, with hands folded in laps. They proceed in pantomime.
HOST:
1. Graciously folds napkin and gently wipes teacup.
2. Scoops two spoons of tea leaves into the cup.
3. Stirs tea leaves with stirrer.
4. Pours hot water into the cup.
5. Turns the cup three times in hand, leans a little forward to GUEST and serves the tea.
GUEST:
1. Takes the teacup in hand, takes a small sip in appreciation, and then finishes drinking the tea.
2. Returns the cup graciously to HOST. HOST and GUEST exchange greetings, bowing to one another and ending the ceremony.

Try This
- Pantomime the customs of other countries, especially with children of varied ethnic and cultural backgrounds.

The key game
The ability to concentrate is the key to this creative activity.

Preparation: Talk with class about the importance of concentration and why we need to be quiet and attentive in order to concentrate.

1. Circle formation. One child volunteers to stand in the middle of the circle with eyes closed or blindfolded.

2. The rest of the children sit in the circle and pass a set of keys quietly and continuously from one player to the next.

3. When the teacher (or child leader) snaps fingers, the passing of keys stops abruptly. The last child holding the keys walks quietly up to the blindfolded child without jiggling the keys.

4. The child in the center points to where he thinks he or she hears the sound of the approaching player. If the guess is correct, the approaching player becomes the new "It." If the child with the keys tags the child in the center before being pointed to, "It" remains in the center. The keys are passed around again, repeating same steps.

Try This
- Do a variation in which the blindfolded child standing in the center of the circle holds onto the keys at the beginning of the game. A child sitting in the circle says, "Bring the keys to me." Child in the center listens attentively to the direction of the voice, tries to locate the person, and hands over the keys if the guess is correct. New player with keys becomes "It."

Explain the sport
An experience in sequencing and working with details.

Preparation: Briefly review with children some of the steps in playing a game or sport. Make a list of the steps.

1. Divide the class into four groups.

2. Each group must carefully explain to the other three groups how a particular sport or game is played. The "catch" (or challenge) is that the explanation must be done *without* talking.

Try This
- Explain in pantomime an important historical event
- Pantomime how a computer game is played.
- Pantomime what tomorrow's weather will be.
- Pantomime the recipe for a favorite dish.
- Pantomime the directions from home to school.

Mystery box

A good game to develop imagination, observation, and sense of touch.

Preparation: Prepare a medium size cardboard box, decorate it, and cut a hole into the top large enough to fit a pair of hands. Fill the box with objects of varying shape, texture, and size.

1. Have children sit on the floor facing the box.

2. Inform children that there are several small objects in the box. A volunteer will reach into the box, grasp one object, feel it, identify it (but will not reveal what it is to others). The object is then left in the box.

3. The child then pantomimes what he or she felt in the box (child may also make sounds as hints), and the other children guess what it is.

Try This

- Use objects to teach home economics, such as a spoon, fork, measuring cup, wash cloth, sponge, or any other kitchen item that is not sharp or dangerous.
- Relate the objects to personal hygiene lessons by using soap, a toothbrush, tube of toothpaste, a sponge, nailbrush, or any other small object related to the subject.
- Use objects to gain experience in contrasting texture (rough-smooth), weight (heavy-light), and so on.

Seasons

Younger children associate specific times of the year with memorable events such as birthdays, summer vacations, Christmas, and so on. This is a perfect way to acquaint children with the seasons.

1. Draw a snowman (winter) on the blackboard, a flower bud beginning to open (spring), sun and beach umbrella (summer), and leaves falling off a tree (fall). Feel free to use whatever you associate with the seasons. You might use posters or large pictures from magazines instead of drawings.

2. Divide the class into four groups; each group will be assigned one season.

3. Tell each group that everyone will have a chance to pantomime individually anything associated with that season. Three groups will watch while the members in one group perform.

4. After each individual pantomime, the children guess the seasonal activity that was represented.

5. After each performance, ask the child what he or she especially likes about that season and why.

Magic motions

It's always fun to change an object into something else. This role-playing game is good for developing spontaneity.

Preparation: Think and talk about the word "change" and how we can change things, depending on how we use them.

1. Have children sit in a circle.

2. Toss a rolled-up scarf to a player to start the game.

3. The player changes the scarf into an object and becomes a character doing something with the object. Examples: cape and matador, baby and mother, napkin and waiter, and so on.

4. After awhile, the teacher or leader rings a bell. This signals the player to toss the scarf to someone else; game continues.

Try This

• Play the game as a part of a history lesson (pick a favorite period), or geography lesson (characters and objects from different countries), or as part of your language arts lesson.

• Use a cardboard box instead of a scarf. Upon signal, player *hands* box to someone else.

Pantomime proverbs

It's fun to act out famous sayings, especially in silence.

Preparation: Have the children collect a number of proverbs that interest them: "A friend in need is a friend, indeed;" "Look before you leap!" or, "A watched pot never boils." Write the proverbs on separate slips of paper and place them in a hat or bowl.

1. Children take turns picking a slip of paper from the hat.

2. One at a time, children pantomime the proverbs. When each pantomime is concluded, the rest of the children can take turns guessing it.

3. If desired, the child performing may ask another child or two to help pantomime the proverb (two children join hands to make a river, while the third child looks before leaping over it).

Try This

• Work out pantomimes to go with the holidays. For example, slips of paper might be placed in a Jack-O-Lantern at Halloween time. They might read, "You are a scarecrow shaking in the wind." Or, "You are a witch riding a broom."

Look at me

Everyone can learn the names of class members in a creative way. This game is especially good for the first week of school.

Preparation: Everyone sits in a big circle. Children take turns announcing their full names.

1. Remaining in circle, children recite this simple rhyme:

Look at me, look at me
Tell me what you can see—
Is it me, is it me
Or is it *(pantomime action)* that you see?

2. The rest of the group tries to guess what the action is and the character.

3. The child who guesses correctly becomes "It."

4. The group recites the rhyme again, and the child who is "It" performs a new pantomime. Game continues in same manner.

Try This

• Explore specific character roles: historical figures, community helpers, storybook figures, nursery rhyme characters, and so on.

Clay creatures

It's fun to combine two or more artistic expressions. This game imaginatively integrates the arts of clay-making and pantomime.

1. Children make different shapes with their bodies.

2. Using these shapes to trigger ideas, the children mold all different kinds of objects from clay—abstractions, animals, and so on.

3. The children place these objects in different positions, thus creating little scenes made up of clay pieces.

4. Using the clay scenes as an inspiration, groups of children can now create similar scenes with their bodies.

Try This
• Create seasonal scenes, scenes from history, farm life, city life, and so on.
• Add music or sounds during any part of the creative process.

Notes

SPEAK UP!

Of tragedies and treasures,
Of paupers and kings...
Words can tell us
About so many things!
We all have things to tell
That come from deep inside.
When we feel free to speak
Words are on our side.

City sounds

This game gives each player an opportunity to develop concentration; also an exercise on following instructions.

1. Select a group of 8-10 players. Remaining children will be observers.

2. Group is asked to think of sounds associated with living in the city (examples: fire engines, sirens, garbage trucks, train whistles).

3. Player who thinks of an associated sound will represent that sound.

4. Arrange group with four people sitting in a row, and four people standing directly behind the seated players.

5. Leader stands in front of group with a sheet of paper which has a chart showing the placement of each player and each player's sound.

6. Players are given instructions to watch the leader. Raising the hands may mean "louder," finger to lips, "softer," a sweep of the leader's hand, "all together."

7. Upon signal, each player chants his or her word or sound rhythmically with the rest of group. The leader may signal volume, tempo, or silence. In this way the whole activity is orchestrated and the students are, in fact, acting like instruments.

Try This
• Use sounds of the beach, jungle, barnyard, or zoo.

Story sculpture
This game motivates children to use their imaginations and creativity.

Preparation: Have class review scenes and images from well-known stories, such as Tom Sawyer painting a fence, Harriet Tubman leading slaves to freedom, Homer Price running his doughnut machine.
1. Divide class into four or five groups.
2. Each group decides on a scene from a story familiar to the class that it would like to portray.
3. Two or three members in each group sculpt the scene (or image) using the bodies of the rest of the children in the group.
4. The "frozen" sculpture slowly comes to life and the characters ad lib the dialogue of the scene.

Try This
• Bring prints of famous paintings to class to be studied and then sculpted. Take snapshots of your living sculptures! Sculpt historic moments.

Pet parade
It's fun to mime animals and to learn classmates' names at the same time.

Preparation: Have children examine pictures of different animals and identify them.
1. Players sit in a circle.
2. First player says, "I went to the Pet Parade and took along my————,"and mimes an animal whose name begins with the first letter of his or her name. Example: Milton says, "I went to the Pet Parade and took along my (he mimes a mouse)."
3. Other children guess what the pet is *(Milt~ mouse)*.
4. Game continues with players taking turns miming and guessing the animals and names. Add sounds only if necessary.

Try This
• Add what each pet likes to do at the Pet Parade: *Milton's mouse moves, Jack 's jackal jiggles.* Put on circus music and have a parade with the animals marching around the room.

Back-to-back
Children can compare nonverbal and verbal modes of expression.

Preparation: Ask children, "How can we communicate ideas about the same subject with words and then without words?" Conduct a short discussion (you might want to teach some hand signs at this time), and then announce, "Let's play Back-to-Back!"

1. Divide the class into two long lines (count off by ones and twos) standing back-to-back.

2. Decide with class on a simple, two character role-playing situation; for example, two members of a family arguing over who should get to eat the last apple in the fruit bowl (or have a prepared list of role-playing situations to use).

3. Players now turn around and face each other. The first time around, the scene is pantomimed. The second time around, use speech and a few props, if desired.

4. Players compare scenes and then think of a new theme for the next round of Back-to-Back.

Try This
• Act out Back-to-Back historical scenes or current news items.

Stop 'n' go stories
Children are challenged to think spontaneously as they enact suggested story ideas.

1. Divide class into groups of five. Choose a director for each group. The director's job is to assign roles and provide a general setting (example: a farmer, his wife, and their two children getting ready to eat dinner).

2. After this is done, the director starts and stops the acting from time to time and asks members of the audience what it wants to see happen next. The actors pick up immediately on the suggestions and continue the action. Director repeats the process until finally asking the audience how it would like to see the story concluded.

Try This
• Act out different kinds of Stop 'n' Go Stories: action adventure, a comedy, detective story, ghost tale, and so on.

Behind the scenes

Children will develop confidence and learn to project their voices when given frequent opportunities to speak before a group of classmates.

Preparation: Brainstorm with children original ideas for television shows and commercials. Put the following words (and those of your own choosing) on separate large sheets of oaktag or cardboard: *louder, softer, faster, slower, more expression.*

1. Have the class divided into small groups. Choose one of the groups to be "studio personnel." Ask the other groups to create a short scene or commercial to be shown on television.

2. As the other groups take turns "broadcasting" their scenes, the studio personnel is in charge of modulating the voices of performers. They hold up appropriate signs to direct the acting. Performers must make an effort to follow through on the suggestions of the studio personnel.

Try This

• Play back scenes in slow motion, roll scenes forward, freeze frames. Or, create TV panels with famous "authorities" and TV quiz shows (good for incorporating spelling, math, and social studies lessons).

Commercials

Day and night we're bombarded with television commercials. Here's a chance for players to get even and make up their own. Promotes teamwork, clear speaking, and voice control.

1. Divide the class into four or five groups of about five players each.

2. Each group thinks of something it would like to sell and takes about 20 minutes to work out a 30-second commercial.

3. As guidelines, each member of the group should know WHO he or she is; WHAT he or she is doing in the commercial; and WHERE the commercial takes place. After the first series of commercials, try the activity again, increasing the length of time to 60 seconds.

4. Check: Are the performers projecting themselves so that they can be seen and heard? Have class members evaluate each performance.

Try This

• Ask for funny commercials; serious commercials; slow-motion commercials; commercials with music or other sounds; commercials promoting travel, new inventions, favorite toys, sports equipment.

Who am I and what am I doing?

A good way to introduce pantomiming to children. Also encourages children to speak in complete sentences.

1. Teacher stands in front of class, pretends to blow a whistle, and motions with hands as if directing traffic. Children guess who the teacher is miming and what the person is doing. Explain that answers must be given in complete sentences, for example: "Mrs. Jones is a policewoman who is blowing a whistle and directing traffic."

2. Ask for volunteers to mime someone new.

Try This
• Pantomime nursery rhyme characters familiar to the children.
• Work in categories: neighborhood helpers, school workers, hospital workers, zoo animals.

Syl-la-bles

A different kind of scavenger hunt! Children search for syllables and put them together to form words.

Preparation: Print a number of words (use words that can be easily acted out: running, jumping, yawning) in big block letters on construction paper or oak tag. Then cut the words into syllables and place them in different places in the room. Put a bowl of paper clips in a centrally located, easy-to-reach place in the classroom.

1. Announce to class that there will be a Syllable Scavenger Special!

2. Children look for cards and try to put words together.

3. When they form a word, they get a paper clip and clip the syllables together. Children may collaborate or swap syllables.

4. When all syllables are found, children return to seats and take turns saying words they collected aloud and acting out what they say. The child who has found the most words and put them together correctly is the winner.

Try This
• Conduct scavenger hunts for different parts of speech.
• Have children work with partners or teams.
• Make a chart of the words hidden in the scavenger hunt so that children can check spelling as they put syllables together.

Tie it together

Props help children to feel more confident when speaking before a group of classmates.

Preparation: Ask children to bring in various small props (example: comb, book, beads, pipe,

93

and so forth).

    1. Display props on a table.

    2. Children break-up into pairs. Each pair of players selects three props from the table.

    3. Children plan and present short skits which incorporate the three props into the story line. For example, if a group is using a scarf, comb, and pair of glasses as props, children could perform this skit: a poor elderly woman bundled in a scarf is selling combs on a street corner; she bends over, accidentally drops her glasses in the snow, and a wealthy gentleman steps on them as he is walking by. What happens?

Try This

• Vary the number of props used and the number of children in each group.

On the line
Children have to think quickly for this story-telling game!

    1. Divide class into groups of five.

    2. First group to perform goes to front of room and lines up in order. Teacher or leader assigns group a specific place and the name of an object. For example, the place might be a *park* and the object, a *pencil*.

    3. The first player in line starts a story by saying the *first word only,* such as "Once."

    4. Player No. 2 quickly adds the *second word only* to the story: "upon." Player No. 3 jumps in with the *third word:* "a."

    5. In the same rapid fire, the story continues (go back to beginning of line each time last player takes turn) until a whole story spins out. The story must be told nonstop and incorporate the place and object (in this case, a *park* and a *pencil).* If there is too much hesitation between words, the same story must be started again. A story should not exceed two or three minutes.

Try This

• Let each child hold a piece of red paper and green paper. Child who finishes a sentence must hold up the red paper. Child who begins a sentence must hold up the green paper.

I can say it faster than you
Have fun while practicing good articulation.

Preparation: Buy a bag of small party balloons.

    1. Divide children into two equal groups. Have them face each other on opposite sides of the room. In the center of the room mark out a large circle on the floor with chalk. The circle should be large enough to hold two children and one desk.

    2. Have children in both groups count off so that each group member will have a counterpart on the other team.

3. Direct children as follows: "I will say a sentence; everyone must listen carefully. The sentence will not be repeated. When I call a number, both children with the same number will run to the desk in the circle, pick up a balloon, and blow it up. When the balloon breaks, that person must repeat the sentence aloud as clearly and carefully as possible. Whoever says it the most understandably gets a point for his or her team."

Try This
- Call different numbers from each side in the event that the teams are unevenly matched.
- Suggest an interclass contest with a neighboring group.
- Substitute spelling words for sentences, and turn the contest into a spelling bee.
- Add colored crepe armbands for each team so that there might be the "blues" against the "greens."

Notes

LEARNING THROUGH LANGUAGE

There are so many things to remember,
And it all starts the first days of September.
So let's make a game or rhyme of it all,
Never to forget what we first learned in the fall.
"I" before "E," except after "C"—
Now that's a pretty bit of poetry!

What am I thinking of?
Have fun rhyming words with a game that can go on forever!

Preparation: Ask children to name as many objects in the room as possible.

1. Have children sit in a circle.

2. One player goes into the center of the circle and says, "I'm thinking of a word that rhymes with *chair*" (or anything else in the room).

3. Class members take turns pantomiming words which rhyme with chair. For example, one player pantomimes eating a pear.

4. The player in center says, "No, it's not a pear."

5. One at a time, children pantomime their guesses until the right word is hit upon. At that time, player in the center says, "Yes, it is a square."

Try This
- Rhyme words for objects found at the circus, playground, park, and so on.
- Make a chart of all rhyming words named.

Details
This game helps one to develop an awareness of self and others.

1. Children work in pairs. They sit facing each other and take turns describing one another: "I see your dimple, brown eyes, and curly hair."

2. After a few minutes, children stand and take turns describing each other's clothing, jewelry, and so on. Encourage children to start sentences with, "I see——————,"

3. Children switch partners several times.

4. After awhile everyone joins in a big circle. Talk about the need for concentration when trying to observe details. Have children mention some details they noticed for the first time.

Try This
- Pass around many different objects and have children describe them in detail. After a few minutes, put away the objects and have children recall as many objects and details as possible.
- Observe details in the room (everyone can put on his or her "super-sight glasses"). Make a list of these details.
- Have children draw pictures of their partners. Ask them to notice as much detail as possible. Make a list of the details that should be included in their portraits.

Story characters
An interesting drama game that uses children's knowledge of fairy tales.

Preparation: Have children talk about their favorite fairy-tale characters.

1. Children walk quietly around the room as teacher beats a drum softly.

2. When the beating stops, the children quietly find a partner.

3. Teacher calls out the title of a familiar fairy tale, legend, or folktale. After a brief consultation, the partners agree upon two characters from the named story that they will represent. They may use sound, movement, or mime to show who they are. The noise level should be kept down so that all partners can perform simultaneously.

4. After a few minutes, the drum beating starts again, and teacher names a new story. Again, children walk around quietly until the drum stops. They choose different partners and assume new roles.

5. Game continues in the same manner.

Try This
• Substitute well-known contemporary characters for fairy-tale characters; mix classical and contemporary characters such as Robin Hood and the mayor of your town.

Add a plural
Watch the sentence grow—a new way to practice grammar rules!

1. Children sit in two lines facing each other.

2. Explain that they will be working with sentences that contain plurals (or any other grammar topic). For example, "The cats are on the rugs."

3. The children are given the sentence to repeat. The first child in each line adds a plural word or phrase to the sentence. For example, "The cats are on the rugs eating snacks." The next child adds still another plural word or phrase. The sentence continues to grow as the sentence is passed down the line. The group which has the fewest mistakes is declared the winner.

Try This
• Make sentences and add verbs in the past tense, future, and so on.
• Whisper a sentence to the first student in each line and have that student whisper it to the next person in line. The sentence is passed down the two lines in the same way. The children then compare the sentences of the last members of each line to see which team has the most accurate version of the original sentence.

Mix and match
Children learn to construct simple sentences.

Preparation: Decorate several medium-size cardboard boxes. Cut a hole into the top of each to fit a child's hand or a 3" x 5" index card. Now, put several index cards together and write a sentence, using one card per word as shown:

Shuffle the cards and put them into one of the boxes. Repeat the procedure for several sentences.

1. Divide the class into groups of three or four.

2. A box is given to each group. Each child removes one card from the box and places it on the table. Then they try to arrange the cards so that a sentence is formed.

3. When the complete sentence is formed, the cards are returned to the box. Teacher rotates boxes to different groups. The procedure is repeated.

Try This
- Use a picture story. Children arrange pictures in sequence as they draw picture cards from box.
- Use two sets of animal pictures per box and have children match them as they withdraw the pictures (match kitten and cat, pony and horse, calico cat and Persian cat, shepherd dog and collie, and so on).

Pass the ball
Who knows what will happen next in this storytelling game?

1. Divide class into five groups, with approximately five players each.

2. Each group sits in a circle.

3. In each group, a ball is passed to one of the players. This player starts a story, "Once upon a time, there was a —————," and continues to tell a story for 20 seconds or so.

4. Player passes the bail to another player in the circle who must continue the story. The story-building continues until everyone has had a turn.

Try This
- Have someone in each group summarize the completed story.
- Tell familiar as well as original stories in the circle.
- Act out parts of the story as it is told.
- Act out a complete story after it is told.

The homophone game

Children learn different spellings of words that sound the same, but have different meanings.

1. Ask for a volunteer to go to the chalkboard. Volunteer will write down all dictated messages.

2. Ask for another volunteer. Hand this person a slip of paper on which a set of homophones is written. Explain that the homophones must be used in a telephone message to Volunteer No. 1.

3. Volunteer No. 2 mimes a telephone call to Volunteer No. 1. The dialogue might go something like this:

No. 2: Hello, This is Mrs. Gaddis. Is your mother home?

No. 1: (at chalkboard) No, she isn't...

No. 2: I have an important message. Will you please write it down?

No. 1: Yes, Mrs. Gaddis!

No. 2: Here's the message: *"Principal* Gaddis called. At tonight's PTA meeting, the *principle* reasons for the sports program will be discussed."

4. After Volunteer No. 1 writes the message on the chalkboard, the rest of the class decides if the correct spellings have been used for the homophones. Corrections are made if necessary.

5. Continue in the same manner, using different volunteers and different sets of homophones each time.

Spelling puzzles

This is a great game for sharing spelling and vocabulary skills.

Preparation: Several sheets of cardboard or oaktag cut into 9" x 14" pieces. Print a vocabulary or spelling word on each piece of board. Then cut the cardboard into two pieces. Examples are shown.

1. Divide class into two even groups. Have each group work within a specific area of the classroom to cut down on confusion and excessive wandering.

2. Distribute the cut-up patterns at random within each group so that each child has part of a

card. Make sure that all parts of any words are distributed within the same group.

3. Children walk around the group trying to match their pieces. When a match is made, the word formed should be read aloud by the players involved.

4. Collect word pieces from each group and redistribute each set to a new group. Repeat step 3.

Try This
- Cut cards into patterns of three or more sections.
- Use phrases or proverbs on the cardboards.
- Teach arithmetic by using equations on cards.
- Teach geography by drawing maps on cardboard pieces.
- Use animal pictures for younger children.

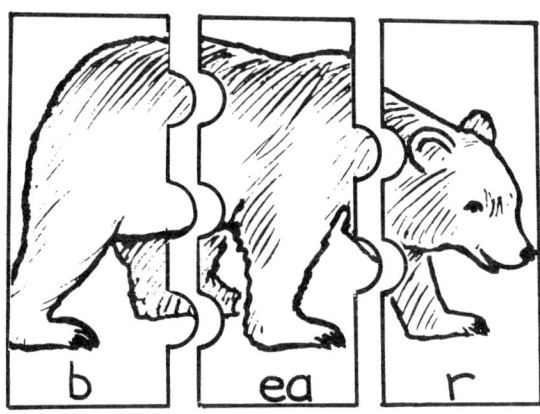

First line, last line
Children have an opportunity to create a short play.

Preparation. Discuss plays. Tell children that a play should have a beginning, middle, and end. Suggest that when they make up a play, they should concentrate on WHO their characters are, WHAT the characters are doing in each scene, and WHERE the action takes place.

You will also need to prepare a list of opening and closing script lines. Write them on individual strips of paper.

1. Divide the class into four groups.

2. Assign each group a *first* line of dialogue and a *last* line of dialogue. The two lines don't have to be related; for example: "My feet ache" and "Look at that beautiful cat!"

3. Each group has fifteen minutes to plan a short skit which starts with the first line and ends with the last line.

4. The skits are then performed for the rest of the class. Tape-record the skits if you wish dialogues to be transcribed.

Definition detectives
Vocabulary grows with this game!

Preparation: Remind the children to have paper and dictionaries handy.

1. Divide the class into four or five groups.

2. First child in each group picks a word from the dictionary. He or she asks everyone in the group to write a definition of the word without looking in the dictionary.

3. After the children read their definitions and compare them, the dictionary definition is read by the child who picked the word. Children correct their definitions if necessary.

4. Second child in each group picks a new word from the dictionary. Repeat steps until everyone in group has had a turn to pick a word.

5. Have each group share its words and definitions with the rest of the class. Let volunteers pantomime the words or use them in sentences that can be acted out.

Try This
- Have children keep a vocabulary notebook for this game.
- Encourage children to look for words in newspapers, magazines, and library books when they are at home. Ask them to take these words out when it's time to play Definition Detectives.

Alphabet lunch
Children have creative fun learning to alphabetize.

Preparation: Recite the alphabet several times with the children.

1. Children sit in a circle.

2. Player 1 says, "I'm going to have an *apple* for lunch," and pantomimes eating it.

3. Player 2 continues, "I'm going to have an *apple* and *bread,*" and pantomimes taking a bite from both foods.

4. Player 3 continues, "I'm going to have an *apple,* a piece of *bread,* and some *cucumbers.*" The game continues through the alphabet and around the circle. Have a prize for the player who eats *zucchini squash!*

Try This
- Children can draw pictures of objects named.

Add a word
Great for building vocabulary while stimulating the imagination.

1. Children sit in a circle.

2. First player says, "I'm an *athlete* (or any word that begins with *a*)," pantomimes an athlete, and continues with "and I'm looking for my *ball* (any word that begins with *b*)."

3. Next player says, "I'm a *ball* (pantomimes a ball), and I'm looking for a *catcher* (any word that begins with *c*).

4. Game continues through the entire alphabet.

Try This

• Go around the circle with random nouns. For example, "I'm a *dancer* and I'm looking for my *slippers*. I'm a *slipper* and I'm looking for *a foot.*"

LET'S FIND OUT

Did you ever think that you would like to be
A knight-in-armor or a captain-at-sea?
And did you ever wonder what you would would do,
If a major decision were all up to you?
Then fly through time and find a new land—
Pick the people, the places and take a stand!

Reactions

An interesting and fun way to explore what one's actions and reactions might be in an unpredictable situation.

1. Create a setting or situation. For example, a crowded subway car can be represented by arranging chairs or benches in a trainlike manner.

2. Choose a group of 10-12 children to participate in the activity. The rest of the class will observe.

3. Distribute about six description cards (those who receive the cards should conceal the content from others). For example, if the subway situation is used, cards might have descriptions such as: "You are an ill-tempered person trying to read the newspaper"; "You are carrying many packages and squeeze into a narrow seat between two people"; "You are a mother with a crying child—no one wants to give you a seat." Make sure there are conductor and motorman cards also.

4. As the train progresses on its journey, the cardholders act out their roles. The rest of the riders are instructed to react as they think they would if found in such a situation.

5. The observers guess the roles and situations after participants have had a good chance to role-play and develop the skit.

Try This

• Create other roles and situations for worthwhile learning experiences.

Book ends

Reading becomes even more fun when stories are acted out!

Preparation. Talk about some favorite storybook characters.

1. Each student chooses one character from a favorite book. Then, have the children line up in three straight lines at back of the room.

2. The first child in each line goes to the front of the room.

3. Teacher suggests an activity such as, "Going on a picnic." Children at the front of the room bring their characters to life and act out the suggested activity. Remind children to talk and move

as their characters would.

4. After awhile, teacher rings a bell and the three performers go to the ends of their lines. The steps are repeated with the next three characters standing in line.

Try This
• Create an informal group of "Library Players" to act out all kinds of stories on a regular basis.

Crystal ball
Children get the opportunity to change history! A creative game that requires critical thinking.

Preparation: Choose any interesting historical event. Teach the lesson as planned. Also have a glass ball, globe-shaped fish bowl, or any other glass dome available.

1. At the end of the lesson, discuss the most outstanding points of the lesson with the children. Let them discover the turning points of the event. For example: Columbus decides to continue sailing for a few more days despite the crew's fear and suspected mutiny.

2. After the class agrees on the main points of the lesson, put them on a chart. Now, produce the "crystal ball."

3. Tell everyone that they will discuss the lesson again; this time only the turning points or key points will be touched upon. At this point, teacher chooses one person to look into the "crystal ball." This person proceeds to alter history by changing the facts (encourage a bit of theatrics—magic incantations and such). He or she relates a view of what might have been if key events had been altered or had never taken place.

Try This
• Dramatize the events before and after certain turning points in history.
• Use nursery rhymes with younger children. For example, what might have happened if Jack had *not* climbed the beanstalk?

Geography
A good follow-up activity for a geography lesson.

1. Have children seated in a circle.
2. Decide on a geographical classification: countries, states, or cities.
3. If using cities, the first player may start by naming any city, such as Cleveland. The next person must name a city that begins with the letter D, the last letter of Cleveland. If Duluth is named, the next city must begin with the letter H, the last letter of Duluth. Game continues in this manner.
4. You may wish to set a limit for the amount of time used to think of each new city.

Try This
• Use animal names as a variation with younger children.
• Use any words (no categories) as a basis for a vocabulary lesson.

That is my hat!

A good way to explore answers to the question, "What do you want to be when you grow up?"

Preparation: Students collect an assortment of different hats worn by members of the community. Be resourceful! Children can uncover old hats at home, make hats, or find them at secondhand stores.

1. Divide the class into four or five groups.

2. Each group member chooses a hat and assumes the occupational role associated with the hat. Each group prepares a five-minute skit incorporating the different occupations of its members (if there are not enough hats to go around, have one group work at a time while the rest of the class is engaged in other activities).

3. The skit should have a beginning, middle, and end. Players should concentrate on *who* they are, *what* they want, and *where* the action takes place. There should be a problem or conflict that needs to be solved.

4. After each performance, have the entire class discuss the skit:

(a) What was the main problem or conflict?

(b) What was each person's role in the conflict?

(c) How was the problem solved? In what other ways could the problem have been solved?

(d) What happened at the beginning, middle, and end?

Scrambled sentences

Children practice proper speech patterns.

Preparation: Teacher writes a scrambled sentence on the chalkboard.

1. Leader assigns each word of the scrambled sentence to a different student (assign the period also).

2. The selected students go to the front of the room and arrange themselves in grammatical order. For example, the words *ran, today, The, to, slowly, bear,* and *cave* could be unscrambled to become, "The bear ran slowly to the cave."

3. Students take turns acting out the unscrambled sentence.

Try This
• Divide words into syllables, and then scramble. Assign each syllable to a different student. Repeat steps above.
• Have children write their assigned words or syllables on individual slates or sheets of paper and

display them to class as they arrange themselves.

Cobalt counter

An exciting game that may motivate a science lesson! All players can participate in this activity directly or indirectly.

Preparation. Assign Space Leader. Also, have a soundmaker handy and a utensil that can be used as a "cobalt counter."

1. The group pretends to be in a space station laboratory, preparing to monitor the blast-off of a manned space rocket.

2. Suddenly, the Space Leader sounds the alarm (bell, buzzer). Space Leader informs the group that radioactive cobalt is missing somewhere in the laboratory. It must be found before the astronauts can take off!

3. The Interstellar Space Commission must use the special "cobalt counter" to locate the missing substance.

4. Space Leader chooses a player to be Mission Leader. He or she is given a pair of castanets, finger cymbals, or other soundmaker. The Mission Leader picks an Inspector who must leave the room with the "cobalt counter." While the class watches, the Mission Leader hides the object designated as cobalt.

5. The Inspector is then asked to return to the room to search for the cobalt. The Mission Leader beats a loud, fast rhythm on the soundmaker as the Inspector gets closer or hotter on the trail, and a softer, slower rhythm as the Inspector gets farther away from the missing cobalt.

6. If the Inspector finds the cobalt, he or she may become the new Space Leader. If he or she does not locate it, then present Space Leader chooses a successor.

Try This

• Apply this game principle to an Easter egg hunt or a treasure hunt with several objects hidden away.

• Modify it to a science lesson in which other mysterious substances are lost.

108

Drama detectives

Children integrate the processes of reading, acting, and writing.

Preparation. Have the class read a story together.

1. After children have completed the story, write the following questions on the chalkboard or chart paper (highlight the initial W's):

Magic W's
Who is the central character?
What does he or she want in the story?
Who gets in the way of this goal? Why?
Where does the story take place?
When does the story take place?

2. Divide class into groups of five or six. Each group will create and enact its own play, using the Magic W's as a guide. Encourage the students to be come nosy "Drama Detectives" who ask as many questions as possible about the Magic W's. Once they have all the answers to the Magic W questions, they can begin to put the information together in play form.

3. Each group performs its version of the story.

4. After each group has had a chance to perform, several students in each group can take turns writing out the dialogue.

Discoveries

Children learn the names and characteristics of many animals. A good group game for a rainy day!

Preparation: Have plenty of animal, bird, and fish books available for children to browse through.

1. Divide class into four groups. Name one person Chief Forest Ranger.

2. Each group counts off so that all players have counterparts on the other teams. Each group chooses a team captain.

3. The Chief Forest Ranger calls a number while sitting at the front of room. All players with that number go to the front and Chief Forest Ranger whispers the name of an animal, bird, or fish to each of them. These players return to their groups and pantomime whatever animal has been assigned.

4. Questions are permitted to help the groups guess the animal. However, the performer is not allowed to speak; he or she may only gesture to give clues. Team captains consult with their groups before guessing the name of the animal. The first team which guesses correctly scores a point. The Chief Forest Ranger then selects another number and the name is repeated.

Passport

An excellent motivation or follow-up activity for a geography lesson. Children get the chance to assume adult roles.

Preparation: Children make passports by folding cardboard or oak tag into 3" x 6" folders. They may bring in photos to paste into their passports, and decorate the covers with "official" emblems. Vary "nationalities" among the passports. This would be a good time to bring a real passport to class. Talk about the information contained, and the reasons such information is necessary. Teacher chooses several children to be Inspectors before activity starts.

1. At an area designated as "Customs," Inspectors examine passports, compare pictures to the holders, and stamp passports (any rubber stamp will do nicely). Players board a ship (group of rearranged chairs) after passing through Customs successfully.

2. Players get off the ship and go through Customs once more after they have landed in a "foreign" country. They show their passports and have them stamped again. This time there is a language barrier which the Inspectors impose by speaking in gibberish or nonsense syllables. The travelers do not understand what the Inspectors say and try to communicate nonverbally.

Try This
- Travelers are met by children costumed in native dress when they debark. Use the library to research the costumes.
- Cook an ethnic food for all the children to sample (parents may be involved in this activity).
- Play games of the foreign country being visited. Again, use the library!

Now, with the pantomime and verbal skills you have learned, you have earned a Passport for your many creative journeys ahead. Have a wonderful time!

More Monologues and Scenes from PLAYERS PRESS

SHORT SCENES FROM SHAKESPEARE, vol 1 by Samuel Selden & William-Alan Landes
Two to ten minute monologues and scenes from the best of Shakespeare with introductions, staging notes and diagrams. Ideal for classrooms and workshops. **144 pgs   pb   5.5x8.5   ISBN 0-88734-632-4**

SCENES FOR ACTING AND DIRECTING by Samuel Elkind
176 pp pb 6x9
Scenes from classic and modern plays, ideal for auditions and workshops.
Vol. 1 ISBN 0-88734-617-0   **Vol. 2** ISBN 0-88734-623-5

HUMOROUS MONOLOGUES by Vernon Howard
Fifty, fresh, wholesome, original and amusing monologues, for either sex, that are ideal for audition or presentation. They are approximately three to five minutes in length. Some of the monologues can easily be cut for shorter use.   **128 pgs.   5.5x8.5 pb ISBN 0-88734-667-7**

MONOLOGUES FOR TEENS by Vernon Howard
Forty, bright, wholesome, new monologues of various lengths. They cover subjects that teenagers are interested in, such as romance, the first job, learning to drive, playing the piano, exaggeration, flying, clubs, beauty treatments, etc.   **128 pgs pb 5.5x8.5 ISBN 0-88734-666-9**

HARPER CHRONICLES, THE by Al Schnupp
Thirty-five flexible monologues (14m, 15f, 6m/f.) Stand alone audition or workshop pieces, one to four minutes, some interrelated to extend their length. A delightful comic gathering of poignant memories and quirky characters.   **68 pgs pb 5.5x8.5 ISBN 0-88734-264-7**

ABSURD, BLACK AND COMIC SKETCHES by Peter Joucla
Fifteen exciting comic monologues and duologues, with director's notes. Ideal for teens, with an equal amount of male and female parts.   **64 pgs.   pb 6x9   ISBN 0-88734-613-8**

GIRL'S NIGHT OUT by Judith Prior
A series of ten sidesplitting skits and sketches for women. These skits are simple to stage, broadly humorous, occasionally outrageous, and the perfect way to break the ice to a perfect entertainment or audition.   **pb 5.5x8.5 ISBN 0-88734-019-9**

NEW WORKS FOR READER'S THEATRE
Terrific new scenes by five American Playwrights. "...widely varied collection designed specifically for readers theatre...standout pieces...clever...funny..." BOOKLIST   **112 pgs 6x9 ISBN 0-88734-644-8**

NEW MONOLOGUES FOR READER'S THEATRE
An exciting collection for young people and adults! This is the companion to the above book. Endorsed by: Salem Ludwig, Actors Studio/HB Studio— "Extremely well written."; Anne Jackson and Eli Wallach—"we heartly recommend this collection." "...new material for every age and many moods. If you are a dramaturge looking for monologue books to recommend, keep this one in mind." ACADEMIC LIBRARY BOOK REVIEW   **112 pgs 6x9 ISBN 0-88734-651-0**

Available at your Local Book Store or directly from:
PLAYERS PRESS, P.O. Box 1132, Studio City, CA 91614-0132 U.S.A.

Theatre Games, Scenes, Monologues and Improvisation
from PLAYERS PRESS

LOOK, LISTEN AND TRUST   by George Rawlins and Jill Rich

Structural material/theatre games to enhance performance and social skills This book is ideal for High School teachers and students.   It offers and excellent selection of new games and details the presentational techniques.   **192 pgs.   pb   5.5x8.5   0-88734-618-9**

PLAYING THE GAME   by Christine Poulter

100 step-by-step theatre games that can be used to develop acting, social and personal skills. This carefully divided book gives games in groups and quickly outlines the material. This is a workbook that can be simply put to work.   **160 pgs.   pb   5.5x8.5   0-88734-611-1**

PERFORMANCE ONE by William-Alan Landes

A wide range of superb monologues for women, focusing on life's intense moments. Flexible lengths, from one to four minutes. Variable age ranges. Each monologue has a detailed introduction to set the moment and help prepare the character. Excellent for auditions, workshops and classroom use. "Some of the very best monologues... A gem of a collection for women. A rare acting book that should be required reading." SHOWCASE   **128 pgs. pb 5.5x8.5 ISBN 0-88734-122-5**

FUNNY SKITS AND SKETCHES by Terry Halligan

Short comic skits and funny sketches. Use each skit by itself, for class or workshop exercises, or string several of them together, add some music and you have a great show.   Ideal for all ages. Easy to memorize and great for ad libs.   **128 pgs. pb 5.5x8.5 0-88734-688-X**

MOMENTS by David Crawford

Sixteen highly compelling duet scenes for men and women; some from new plays. Carefully selected to provide the complete moment of action with a strong emphasis on character relations. Each scene is prefaced with a brief synopsis of the play and character descriptions. They can be simply, easily and effectively presented.   **pb 5.5x8.5 ISBN 0-88734-664-2**

MONOLOGUES AND SCENES FROM WORLD THEATRE by William-Alan Landes, ed.
pb 5.5 X 8.5 (...quality selection... SHOWCASE)

Monologues and Scenes, collected and cut from the finest classic plays in world literature. Each with a brief introduction providing general background and detail for understanding the characters. Production notes, in the margins, are written to stimulate the actor and encourage the director.

Vol. 1 — Ancient Greek & Roman	0-88734-125-X
Vol. 2 — German, French, Italian, Spanish, Russian	0-88734-126-8
Vol. 3 — Belgian, Austrian, Scandinavian, Irish	0-88734-127-6
Vol. 4 — English	0-88734-128-4
Vol. 5 — American	0-88734-129-2
Vol. 6 — Shakespeare	0-88734-130-6

Available at your Local Book Store or directly from:
PLAYERS PRESS, P.O. Box 1132, Studio City, CA 91614-0132 U.S.A.